# NIGHTHAWK ONE

## Recollections of a Helicopter Pilot's Tour of Duty in Northern Ireland during the Troubles

Peter Shaw

Helion & Company

Helion & Company Limited
Unit 8 Amherst Business Centre
Budbrooke Road
Warwick
CV34 5WE
England
Tel. 01926 499 619
Email: info@helion.co.uk
Website: www.helion.co.uk
Twitter: @helionbooks
Visit our blog at blog.helion.co.uk

Published by Helion & Company 2023
Designed and typeset by Mary Woolley (www.battlefield-design.co.uk)
Cover designed by Paul Hewitt, Battlefield Design (www.battlefield-design.co.uk)

Text © Peter Shaw 2023
Images © as individually credited

Every reasonable effort has been made to trace copyright holders and to obtain their permission for the use of copyright material. The editors and publisher apologise for any errors or omissions in this work and would be grateful if notified of any corrections that should be incorporated in future reprints or editions of this book.

ISBN 978-1-804512-40-1

British Library Cataloguing-in-Publication Data.
A catalogue record for this book is available from the British Library.

All rights reserved. No part of this publication may be reproduced, stored in a retrieval system, or transmitted, in any form, or by any means, electronic, mechanical, photocopying, recording or otherwise, without the express written consent of Helion & Company Limited.

For details of other military history titles published by Helion & Company Limited contact the above address, or visit our website: http://www.helion.co.uk.

We always welcome receipt of book proposals from prospective authors.

*I know that I shall meet my fate*
*Somewhere among the clouds above.*
*Those that I fight I do not hate,*
*Those that I guard I do not love.*
*My country is Kiltartan Cross,*
*My countrymen Kiltartan's poor,*
*No likely end could bring them loss*
*Or leave them happier than before.*
*Nor law, nor duty bade me fight,*
*Nor public men, nor cheering crowds,*
*A lonely impulse of delight*
*Drove to this tumult in the clouds.*
*I balanced all, brought all to mind,*
*The years to come seemed waste of breath,*
*A waste of breath the years behind*
*In balance with this life, this death.*

*An Irishman Foresees His Death*
**W B Yeats (1919)**

# Contents

| | | |
|---|---|---|
| Prologue | | vi |
| List of Abbreviations | | viii |
| Introduction | | x |
| 1 | South Armagh: Bandit Country | 12 |
| 2 | Spinning Up | 23 |
| 3 | Croslieve | 29 |
| 4 | RAF Aldergrove | 32 |
| 5 | Shackleton Shadows | 38 |
| 6 | Bad Guys Rule | 44 |
| 7 | Night Stalkers | 47 |
| 8 | Deadly Down | 56 |
| 9 | All Along the Watchtowers | 61 |
| 10 | Cullyhanna | 70 |
| 11 | City Lights | 74 |
| 12 | The Wild West | 82 |
| 13 | Ops Normal | 90 |
| Epilogue, March 2022 | | 94 |
| Appendix: Early Day Motion | | 96 |
| Bibliography | | 97 |

# Prologue

Between February and May 1990, I completed a roulement tour as a helicopter pilot in Northern Ireland at the height of the Troubles. I flew over 100 missions in support of the British Army, the Ulster Defence Regiment, and the Royal Ulster Constabulary in our role to maintain law and order in a country on its knees with fear. I was only one of many pilots from all three services performing a demanding job in difficult circumstances, no doubt a few experiencing more exacting situations than I met during my short tour. I have every respect for what they achieved but they have remained silent. Prior to the later wars in Iraq and Afghanistan, Northern Ireland was regarded as the most dangerous place to fly as a military pilot. I was no stranger to the province having been sent there 10 years earlier in a different role as a military engineer but these four months I describe remain the most intense period of my life to date.

I was trained for a vastly different kind of conflict. One that would be fought in front of the screen division in North Germany as a forward scout pilot reporting the advance of enemy armoured vehicles through the Fulda Gap. Here there was no identifiable enemy, no recognisable uniform or equipment to report back on, no one coherent organisational structure but a war, nonetheless.

This is primarily a book about flying and the experience it gave me, not the politics about which I have no view. What would be the point?

It was difficult. I did not keep a diary, just my logbook and my maps to remind me of friends long since lost, places long since gone. Neat methodical entries, but no description to convey the adventure. I have tried to bring my logbook to life. The views expressed are mine alone and do not necessarily reflect the views of the Army or Her Majesty's Government. Reluctantly I have had to change the names of the characters mentioned in the book who were my colleagues and friends, and the events and incidents described may have happened at differing times. This is a work of creative non-fiction. All the events in this memoir are true to the best of my memory.

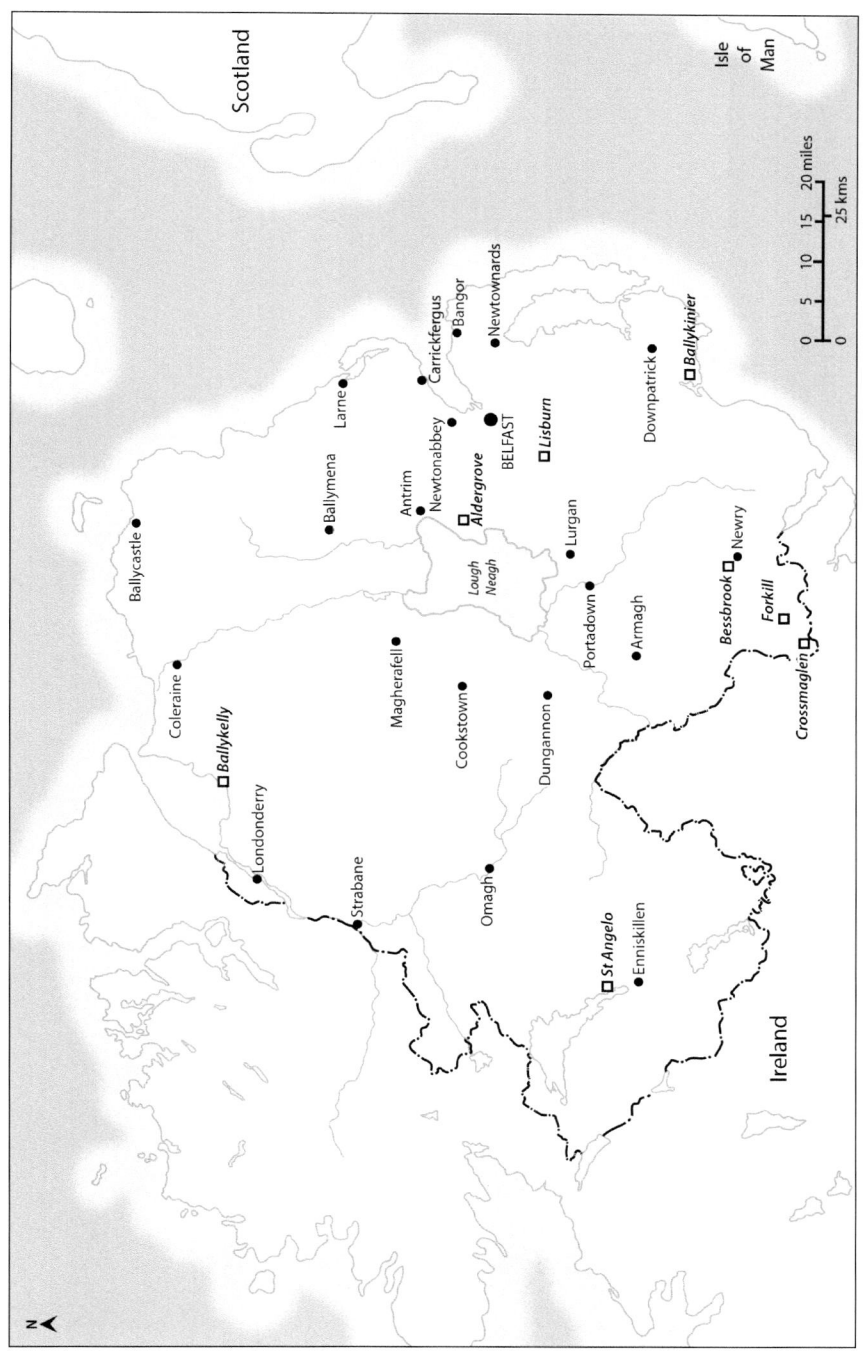

Map of Northern Ireland. (Map by George Anderson)

# List of Abbreviations

| | |
|---|---|
| AAC | Army Air Corps |
| AH | Army Helicopter |
| ASU | Active Service Unit |
| CLF | Commander Land Forces |
| CO | Commanding Officer |
| DShK | Russian-made 12.7mm heavy machine gun |
| HLS | Helicopter Landing Site |
| IRCM | Infrared Counter Measures |
| LCJ | Load Carrying Jerkin |
| LWNA | Lightweight Navigation Aid |
| NVG | Night Vision Goggles |
| OC | Officer Commanding |
| OP | Observation Post |
| PIRA | Provisional Irish Republican Army |
| PVCP | Permanent Vehicle Check Point |
| QHI | Qualified Helicopter Instructor |
| REME | Royal Electrical and Mechanical Engineers |
| RPM | Revolutions per minute |
| RUC | Royal Ulster Constabulary |
| SAM | Surface-to-Air Missile |
| SA80 | (Small Arms for the 1980s) British Army family of weapons |
| SRA | Surveillance Radar Approach |
| TAOR | Tactical Area of Responsibility |
| UDR | Ulster Defence Regiment |
| UHF | Ultra High Frequency |
| VHF | Very High Frequency |
| WO | Warrant Officer |

INTRODUCTION ix

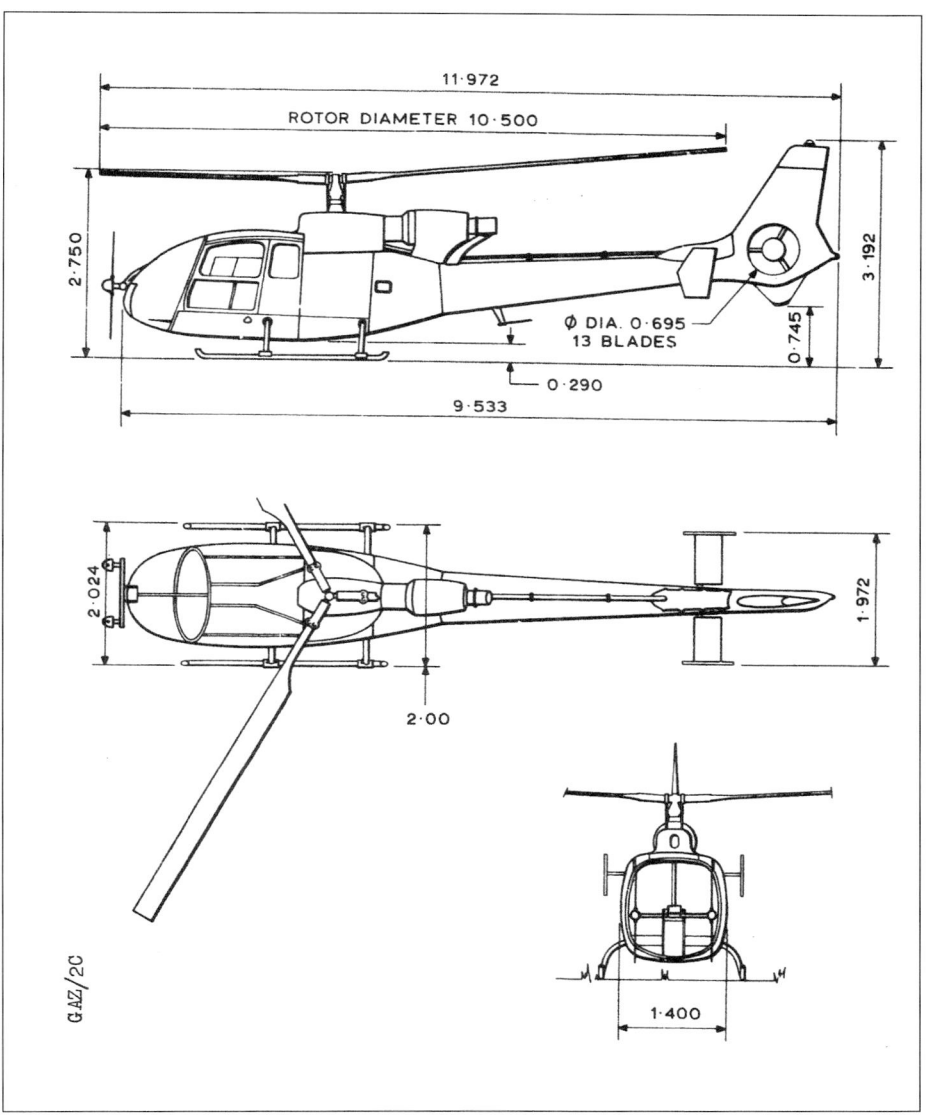

Gazelle outline from Aircrew Manual. (Author's collection)

# Introduction

*It is of importance that we should push on with the practical study of the military use of aircraft in the field and with the training of personnel in observing and conveying information of their observations. I consider that the military personnel employed as observers should also be trained pilots.*

Field Marshall Sir William Nicholson, Chief of the General Staff 1911

My flying ancestors were the Air Battalion Royal Engineers with whom I had the privilege of wearing the same cap badge. The responsibility for military aeronautics in the heyday of 1911 remained in the hands of the Royal Engineers, and the existing Balloon School at Farnborough became the Air Battalion with an establishment of 14 officers and 176 other ranks. They were not all Royal Engineers surprisingly, indeed the No 2 Company, operating flying machines rather than lighter-than-air inventory was commanded by a Captain Fulton in the Royal Field Artillery. The qualifications for those who aspired to fly with the eagles were loosely interpreted as; 'possession of an aviators' certificate, previous experience of aeronautics, good eyesight, good map reader and field sketcher, unmarried, under thirty years of age, a good sailor, a taste for mechanics and of light weight (under 11 ½ stone)'.

Achieving the aviator's certificate issued by the Royal Aero Club was no mean feat, costing £75 – equivalent to around £8,900 today – and it is no wonder that pilots were drawn from the officer class who attended civilian flying schools around the country. In the newly formed battalion, these budding aviators would have been fighting each other to get airborne, however as the unit had precious few planes, either in the stores, unflyable or in the factory being rebuilt or improved after what can only be imagined as frequent clashes with *terra firma*. An order for four Bristol Boxkites, not entirely dissimilar to Cody's Army Aeroplane No 1, improved the situation and the No 2 Company moved to Larkhill on Salisbury Plain, an area where any present-day army aviator is well acquainted. The Company was no fighting force at this stage, much of the flying was learning the characteristics of the diverse types and the gentle art of not crashing, but progress was being made. The Bristol Boxkite was fitted with either the 50hp Gnome or the 60hp Renault air-cooled rotary engine. The Boxkite of that day was not a particularly comfortable conveyance. The pilot sat on the leading edge of the lower plane with his feet on the rudder bar which was supported by an outrigger through which he looked down between his knees into space. The observer sat close behind, and somewhat higher than the pilot with his legs around the latter's body, and he also had a direct view down. The only instruments were an oil-pulsating gauge and an aneroid barometer worn around the neck. Field glasses and an artist's drawing block completed the equipment.

On the 8 June, a significant achievement was the flying of four aircraft to Farnborough at heights of 1,000 to 2,000ft via Andover and Basingstoke, a route I flew on numerous occasions myself 80 years later and I am glad to say also without incident!

Cross-country flying was encouraged to prove efficiency and adventurous contests were entered, many of which were less than successful, however the potential for aircraft to penetrate an enemy's defences from above remained a driving factor in their development.

Towards the end of 1911, due to concern that British military aviation was falling short of their European neighbours – particularly France – a committee was formed to submit its recommendations which ultimately led to the demise of the Air Battalion. It was felt that aviation should be raised in status and become a dedicated organisation outside of the sole control of the Corps of Royal Engineers and drawn from all sources; a view expressed with vigour by no less than Winston Churchill himself. In 1912, the Royal Flying Corps came into being, retaining the Air Battalion as one of the flying companies and now renamed as squadrons to reflect cavalry and naval ambitions. The looming catastrophe of a world war in Europe would soon see this illustrious formation in action, while across the Irish Sea, the seeds of a new rebellion were being sown that would lead to the 1916 Easter Rising, the declaration of a Republic and a new era of Irish nationalism which would eventually lead to the partition of Ireland. Meanwhile, five years earlier, two French brothers had experimented with a revolutionary form of flight of a tethered airframe called Gyroplane No 1 and led to the first manned flight of a helicopter. The story that follows is a direct result of these significant historical events.

# 1

# South Armagh: Bandit Country

## 13 March 1990

It's a chilly March day, and I am sat in the right-hand seat of ZB670 – an Army Gazelle AH Mk 1 – about to fly out of Bessbrook Mill security force base situated on the edge of South Armagh. I have strapped into the armoured seat and stowed my Heckler & Koch 53 automatic rifle into the bracket beside my seat. I reach up and plug my flying helmet into the intercom. A faint whine can now be heard from the main battery through the headset, a prelude to the symphony of familiar sound that will soon be background noise for the next hour.

Outside the helicopter my Aircraft Commander is completing the external checks, the walk round as we call it, I glance to my right where only several metres away and lower down the base sat another army helicopter, a Lynx AH1 at rest, beyond which and lower down still, where the base hardstanding widened out, were a Wessex and a Puma belonging to the RAF. It was unusually quiet this morning considering this was currently the busiest heliport in Europe according to the statistics.

I turn round in my seat to check on our passengers: an RUC sergeant sitting behind me, a real veteran by the look of him, was staring out of the side window bored as if he were on the train to work. Sat next to him fidgeting and clearly nervous is a female constable adjusting her seat straps. I give her a thumbs up and grin. I hadn't managed to talk to them before Staff Newell had strapped them in the back and briefed them, but it looked like this was her first flight down south to the border. She smiled back weakly and looked down. Sliding into the seat next to me, and hooking up his helmet, Newell grinned 'She's probably heard about your flying Sir,' he said on the intercom 'They are going down to start a week's duty, OK we are good to go.'

Shutting his door and once strapped in, my attention moved to the instrument panel and console in front of me. The Gazelle is designed to be flown from the right-hand seat where I am currently sitting as the panel is biased to the right, but with dual controls fitted as standard can be flown from either seat.

We had some checks to do before starting the engine. Releasing the friction on both the cyclic stick and collective levers we checked them for full and free movement both independently and together. I made sure the collective lever was fully down with the friction tight. The landing light switch was set to off and the hydraulic servo switch to ON.

A quick check round the instrument panel and overhead and I was ready to start up. As easy as starting your car, I flicked the start switch on the panel to RUN. The turbine compressor began to spin up powered by the battery and when it reached over 2,000rpm (revolutions per minute), I set the switch to IGNITION and held it here. The whining got louder, and you could begin to hear it through the noise cancelling headset incorporated in my flying helmet. When the temperature of the jet pipe reached an incredible 400 degrees C, the T4, I released the switch back to RUN. The engine would now accelerate by itself to a staggering 25,000rpm and stabilise.

Staff Newell got busy programming the Lightweight Navigation Aid (LWNA). I completed the after start checks which involved more instrument checks and ensuring various warning lights were extinguished and then we could start the rotor. At this point the three rotor blades were braked and locked against turning in the light south-westerly breeze blowing today. I looked up thought the Perspex canopy at the scudding cloudy sky and wondered how many shades of grey were possible today.

Our destination this morning was the joint RUC police station and Security Forces base in the village of Crossmaglen, remarkably close to the border with Ireland. It was only 10 miles away to the south-west but in so many ways it could have been 100. The simple fact was that if the RUC sergeant and his female colleague had tried to drive the short distance to work, they would in all probability not arrive alive. Since 1976, South Armagh had been a no-go area for any kind of vehicle movement. For the Security Forces, to travel by road was a death warrant. These 150 square miles of countryside between Newry and Newtonhamilton to the north and the Irish 'border' to the south were the deadliest in the province. It was not only hostile to movement by road but was increasingly becoming a major problem to flying operations as well.

Our Doppler navigation computer was now programmed and updated with the grid coordinates of Crossmaglen. Apart from this and a marked map of Northern Ireland this was all the navigation aids we had. There was no GPS yet. Dave Newell slewed up both switches to update our reference point here at Bessbrook to increase the accuracy of our position. We were set. I had flown over Crossmaglen a few days earlier from a height but not landed inside. It was going to be interesting.

Thumbs up to the air trooper stood a few metres in front of us with a trolley mounted fire extinguisher by his side, and I switched the anti-collision light on the roof of the cab to ON. One day he would be sitting here I thought. Reaching up with my left hand and keeping my right hand firmly on the cyclic stick, I found the red rotor brake handle, released it, and stowed it fully forward. Next the yellow throttle lever, with the stopwatch running, I advanced it forward an inch or so. The rotor began to turn to the right above my head and the endless whining of the engine increased, the clutch was now engaging the engine with the main gearbox. With a two-stage reduction the gearbox would never turn the rotors anywhere like the speed of the engine which now was also accelerating further, and the machine was now starting to vibrate. With the clutch now engaged, confirmed by the tachometer needles of both the compressor and rotor blades aligned, I continued to advance the yellow throttle forward a couple more inches into the gate making sure I didn't exceed 25 percent on the torquemeter instrument.

By now the helicopter was a screeching, vibrating, low thudding beast. The engine rpm was now fixed above an unbelievable 43,000rpm, while the three-bladed rotor was whizzing above us at 380 revolutions per minute, over six times a second. The noise was unbearable outside the Gazelle, with no ear protection permanent damage to the ear drum would result in less than a minute we were told. Lights out on the Central Warning Panel meant all the oils and electrics were functioning normally, a testament to the incredible servicing and workload regime of the Royal Electrical and Mechanical Engineers (REME) who maintained these amazing machines.

It was time to go.

Dave called it in on Flight Safety Common: 'Red Eight Fifty, Gazelle lifting departing to the south in one minute, Red Eight Fifty.'

I pressed the torquemeter TEST button next to the instrument with my left hand, the over torque warning light illuminated, and the torque indicated zero. Good, the second most important instrument in the cockpit was working.

Hand back on the collective lever on my left I untwisted the friction so that it could be used.

'OK,' I chanted (everything in aviation starts with OK).

'CWP is clear, Ts and Ps within limits, harnesses locked and tight.'

A final nod from Dave, I checked left and satisfied myself we were clear.

Right foot forward on the pedal. Right hand nudging the cyclic stick forward a bit and pull up on the lever a few degrees with my left hand. The helicopter became light on the skids, a burring sound from the rotors and we lifted into an 8ft hover. Lifting the lever with my left hand had made the magic happen.

Imperceptibly, that action had increased the angle of all three blades 'collectively' and lifted the machine off the deck. The blades had tried to slow down of course as they bit into the air but the engine turning so astronomically fast wouldn't let them and kept them at their governed speed. The torque or twisting moment required to keep the helicopter flying had now increased and registered on the instrument. A quick glance and I clocked the reading, I had more than the 10 percent margin I needed to reach the maximum at 102.5 percent. We could lift vertically and fly out.

Bessbrook helipad is surrounded by grey cover from view fencing, topped with security lighting, cameras and antennas, there were multiple ways to hit things if you weren't careful. But we were careful. Dave repeated the safety call saying we were departing.

I pulled further with the collective lever and rose higher, at the same time easing the pressure on the right pedal allowing the nose of the helicopter to rotate slowly left as we climbed. The blades thudded above asking for more power from the engine as we turned and faced almost 180 degrees from rest.

The giant battleship of Bessbrook Mill was now clearly on my right as we lifted higher. Even our small machine caused a downdraft which shook some pallets lying in the corner of the pad. Dave was following me through on the controls, his feet lightly on the pedals and hands poised like a wicketkeeper ready to pounce and take over should anything happen and happen it could.

The next bit of magic involved the stick in front of me held by right hand.

A mere nudge forward perhaps a centimetre and the rotor disc spinning above tilted forward a small amount. By altering the angle of each blade as it swept round above in sequence, I had altered the pitch of the blade on my side of the machine and lowered the pitch on the blade on the opposite side. Due to a delay this had the effect of the blades rising at the back higher than the blades at the front. So what? So now the tilted rotor disc would propel the machine forward and forward accelerating across the ground. A gusty wind rocked the helicopter, we were gaining speed fast now and I increased power now all the way to the intermediate pitch stops on the lever. No more pitch now just convert power into speed as we transited away over line of trees and the outskirts of Bessbrook.

'Red Eight Fifty' was the codeword for Bessbrook Mill helicopter base. The mill was an old linen factory dating from the eighteenth century around which Quaker John Richardson built the village of Bessbrook as a home for his workers when he bought the derelict factory in 1845. In the early 1970s it was acquired by the British Army which needed a base close to South Armagh for troops and helicopters. It was more like a prison than a military base. The first time I went there I got lost in its labyrinthine corridors trying to find the Ops Room. The helicopter site was outside the mill across a public road and was a crowded collection of stepped terrace concrete pads lined up inside high surrounding grey fencing and lighting towers.

500ft now and climbing towards Camlough. A small village which marked the edge of bandit country. Camlough Mountain was visible on our left rising to 1,386ft acting as a sentinel overlooking Bessbrook. I knew we had a watchtower OP up there on the north facing slope where all the approaches into Newry were under surveillance. Keeping the main road out of Newry on our left, I kept climbing higher and higher. Our aim was to get to 1,500ft as quickly as possible. Due to the new perceived SAM (Surface-to-Air Missile) threat and the more long-standing HMG (Heavy Machine Gun) armoury now controlled by PIRA, we had to be ultra-smart to stay alive. That meant in effect staying above 1,500ft or ideally 2,000ft in South Armagh if the cloud base allowed, which it frequently didn't, or flying below 150ft fast at low level where aiming and reaction times for the perpetrator were made significantly more difficult and gave us an increased measure of security. Our best rate of climb today at near our maximum weight was 1,250ft per minute so it would only take under a minute to get there. Today we had a cloud base of 1,800ft forecast to lower during the day so at 1,700ft showing on the altimeter, I lowered the nose, banked left and keeping the lever at the pitch stop turned south over bandit country.

The threat level in this part of the province was Severe. Although incidents did occur almost daily, they were of a minor nature and almost inconsequential, but every event was recorded in detail to develop an overall intelligence picture. When a major incident occurred, it always came without warning and with horrific violence in a brief time span. The most recent major incident in the Crossmaglen area was two years ago on 21 May 1988 when a 28-year-old corporal in the Royal Pioneer Corps was killed instantly in an IRA blast about a mile outside Crossmaglen close to the border with County Monaghan. His sniffer dog died also. He was a married man from Lincoln with a three-year-old daughter and tragically was coming to the end of a two-year tour of duty in Northern Ireland. They were checking the area for bombs and weapons, just 36 hours after experts had defused a half-tonne bomb at Glasdrumman nearby. The patrol was on a planned search which had continued for some days and was crossing a field when a device contained in a biscuit tin exploded in a dry-stone wall.

The border between Northern Ireland and the Republic was no more obvious and clearly defined than, say, that between Hampshire and Wiltshire. In places it ran along streams, hedges, the side, or middle of roads, and in some places even the middle of farmyards. One thing that was expressly forbidden was to overfly the Republic, however small an incursion would become a political incident and result in more aggravation.

Camlough lake rippled far below us in the gathering gloom. To the west I could see the cloud base lowering in dark grey sheets. 'Did you call in yet?' asked Staff Newell. As the Aircraft Commander, he had been hands-full monitoring everything else including keeping the two in the back happy, so I selected Tac VHF on my set and keyed the mike on the cyclic stick. 'Zero One Alpha this is Gazelle Four, Ops Normal.'

The Signals trooper back at RAF Aldergrove keyed back an acknowledgement.

Regimental Ops had no real idea of what we were up to apart from these calls which kept them in touch whenever we were airborne or not. Telephone calls from landing sites also kept them up to date as well as Buzzard Ops at Bessbrook, the Signals sergeant who looked after the pad.

We were heading southeast now skirting the massive bulk of Slieve Gullion to our right. At 1,880ft high the summit was now shrouded in swirling cloud.

Slieve Gullion appears in Irish mythology, where it is associated with the Cailleach and the heroes Fionn mac Cumhaill and Cú Chulainn. It dominates the countryside around it, offering views as far away as Antrim, Dublin Bay, and Wicklow on a clear day. An extinct volcano, it was surrounded by a ring dyke known as the Ring of

Gullion, parts of which were sites for the much-hated watchtowers overlooking the border. Flat topped and steep sided, you could land on it if it was ever clear enough to do so. We had decided today to skirt it to the east where the weather was slightly better. Our next major visual landmark would soon be the Forkhill Road and the Newry–Dundalk railway line which my colleague next to me was peering ahead to identify. At two miles a minute, things appeared fast out of the patchwork and Dave asked for 'about 240 degrees, Sir'.

The largest instrument on the panel, the gyro-magnetic compass, supplied magnetic heading indication. The detector unit was actually in the tail boom and the gyroscope itself was behind the instrument spinning away keeping itself upright and oriented. The little indicator at the bottom right of the instrument was bang in the middle where it should have been. A deflection would indicate an inaccuracy of up to four degrees, but not today. We were right on-heading towards our target now only seven short miles away.

We picked up the Forkhill Road and swung right descending to 1,500ft skirting the southern wooded flank of Gullion. We were definitely over bad boy territory now, any problem with the machine and we would force land out of sight of any friendly security asset and hope that a hastily called Mayday with a grid reference would bring help.

The Gazelle had no armament. It was an observation and reconnaissance helicopter, however we the aircrew were armed. We each carried the HK53 automatic rifle with two 25 round magazines of 5.56mm ammunition giving us a total of 100 rounds, enough to provide a mini defence until support troops arrived. One magazine was loaded on the weapon but never made ready to fire. In addition, we each had a Browning 9mm automatic pistol stowed in our LCJ (Load Carrying Jerkin) vest which was worn over our fire retardant flying suits. The HK53 had a retractable stock which shortened its length sufficiently to be fitted into a bracket, muzzle down, next to the armoured seat. Zipped into the front of my LCJ vest and easily removed was a ceramic one-inch-thick chest protector that extended from under your chin to above your groin. It would protect you from blast fragmentation and low velocity small arms fire but not much more.

Part of the fatigue induced during a working day was the effort involved in wearing all this clobber of equipment which limited your movement inside, especially leaning forward to complete a task, but I still was glad that the money had been spent to give us some measure of protection in this highly hostile area.

Door guns were just starting to be fitted to our Lynx AH1 helicopters, however proposed highly restrictive rules of engagement imposed upon the air trooper door gunners meant that it was rarely to be used and was there more for deterrent purposes. Another problem was the door mount and the sight; so trials were still underway to improve these before it could be declared fully operational.

Ahead the terrain flattened out into rolling farmland much like parts of South Devon, and we crossed the Dundalk Road four miles out from Crossmaglen. My colleague had been chatting briefly to the RUC sergeant who was pointing something out near a crossroads on the left side of the aircraft. We were now in sight of the watchtower at Glasdrumman, nicknamed Golf Three Zero, and Dave broke off his chat to call ahead to the base at Crossmaglen on the Cougar secure net to say that were inbound.

Three miles out now approaching from the east we flew over a small lough, and I slowed the helicopter back to 70 knots by lowering the lever a few inches, simultaneously raising the nose to maintain height. We would now have to get down through the dangerous height band of 1,500ft to 150ft as quickly as possible to minimise the effective range of an automatic weapon attack. Another less important consideration was to try and minimise the noise impact of our arrival. The acoustical signature of a helicopter is partly due to the modulation of sound by the relatively slow turning main rotor, known as 'blade slap'. For a typical light helicopter, blade slap occurs during partial power descents when one rotor blade intersects its own vortex system or that of another blade. When this happens, the blade experiences high velocities and rapid angle of attack changes; the latter being the angular difference between the airflow and the blade itself. The maximum sound generated by this effect occurs at airspeeds of 65 to 85 knots and rates of descent between 300 and 600ft per minute.

The quickest way would be to enter autorotation by lowering the collective lever completely and allowing the helicopter to freewheel downwards with the clutch disconnected. This would produce a startlingly steep descent towards the ground but was not authorised other than for training and could produce complications if the recovery was not completed correctly, so a powered descent was our only option.

With the town clearly visible now, Dave completed some landing checks including setting the radar altimeter bug to 150ft, checking that everyone's harnesses were tight and locked, and in turn we lowered the clear visor on our flying helmets. PIRA were not the only threat now as startled birds could also do a world of damage through a Perspex canopy. The radar altimeter measured height above the actual ground rather than altitude above mean sea level indicated on the primary altimeter on the panel. By setting a little yellow index pointer on the side a light would illuminate when the aircraft was below the set height. 'Right Sir down we go and get that light to come on, come back to about 40 knots.'

'Checks complete, call us in please' I replied.

'Red One Fifty, Red One Fifty, two minutes Gazelle landing from the east, Red One Fifty.' A reply came, a Wessex had departed 10 minutes ago to the north, we were cleared in.

Remembering the advice, I had been given to lose altitude rapidly and thereby avoid the zone of effective fire, I lowered the collective almost fully down but keeping enough pitch to avoid disengaging the clutch in autorotation, and the nose pitched down towards the fields at the same time pushing forward on the cyclic to make the flight path even steeper. Turning steeply left through about 90 degrees and then right just had the effect of increasing the rate of descent even more.

Descending quickly now, we crossed the Creggan River which ran through a small village to our right which gave it its name. Through 500ft now and with a rate of descent of 1,000 feet per minute we would hit the ground in 30 seconds. I picked up the line of the Monog Road which ran west into the town.

One hundred feet is about the height of a nine or 10 storey building and you could notice how the aspect of everything changed in relief. Buildings that appeared in plan now had elevation as did small hills and copses of trees. The red light on the radar altimeter flicked on, I went lower still until the outskirts of Crossmaglen were in landscape across the entire bubble canopy. The combined Security Forces/RUC base was on the far side of town just outside the main square, scene of countless shootings and bombings in recent history. Identifiable by a tall communication mast with a red light on top and its grey fences and black towers, it was an ugly addition amongst the terraced housing, industrial buildings and sports field surrounding it. Home to a company of the Scots Guards at this time, about 80 men were living in cramped conditions inside but being inside was infinitely preferable to walking the killing fields outside.

Blades clattering now, I slowed us to a manageable approach speed aiming for a 50ft hover over the landing spot; a white H was drawn where vehicles would have been parked before. Transitioning to a hover meant raising the nose of the machine a fair bit to slow down but today a fresh breeze from the south-west allowed me to maintain a few precious knots of airspeed to transition away should we come under attack or have to abort for any other reason. Past the town square on my left, I caught sight of the Irish tricolour flying from a pole. It's hard to describe the effect that seeing the tricolour had on your psyche. It symbolised enemy alien territory and shouted the message 'YOU DON'T BELONG HERE'. Crossmaglen was still part of the territory of the United Kingdom like it or not, and we were landing.

A guy in full flak protection ran out from a corner of the base and started to wave us down. I was over the fence now at about 25 to 30ft height, no room to go forward anymore, just vertically down now. The helicopter shuddered and whined its protest against the high hover. Down below the high 20 foot fencing we were out of view from the square now and I pedal-turned to the right slightly and both skids contacted the tarmac.

Lever down, friction on, disc level. We were down!

But I was back after 10 years…I was first here as a convoy commander in 1980 as a Royal Engineer subaltern. My transport then was the standard half-ton military Land Rover and it took three hours rather than the 14-minute flight we had just completed.

The construction and later refurbishment of the hardened accommodation at Crossmaglen were both brigade-level operations involving up to nine battalions (Operation Tonnage). Major route clearances had to be undertaken; the route picketed, engineer plant and materials moved in by road; the construction site protected; and everything removed again on completion.

While Dave helped the relieved passengers disembark from the back of the helicopter, I held the rotor disc steady and checked my surroundings. Directly in front of me was the main structure with the Operations Office and the accommodation block attached. On top of the grey slab-like building with no windows, extra mortar-proof protection had been added. To the left and further down the compound stood the main sangar (fortified position) and watchtower. The only way to describe it was a giant pill box on stilts; the stilts in this case being breeze block construction. Painted black at the top it was surrounded by the latest edition of protection, an anti-rocket cage. At the top of the sangar it was possible to observe the street below in both directions and towards the square where a second sangar stood on the corner. This was known as the Borucki Sanger. Named after Private Borucki from the Parachute Regiment who lost his life here a few years ago, the rocket cage seemed to comprise of scaffolding poles connected together with chain link fencing stretched taut around the observation post. There were numerous generators parked around the compound.

Our two passengers hunched down to lower their profile and ran under the spinning rotors towards the accommodation. Turning back towards us, they gave a thumbs up and waved. 'Poor sods', I thought. I didn't want to spend more time here than I possibly had to. Sitting here with the rotors running we were extremely vulnerable to a possible IRA mortar attack. These mortars were all homemade, not the off-your-shelf variety. There was no limit to their ingenuity. Firing a cut down Calor Gas cylinder packed with explosive, they could have a devastating effect. This base was about as fortified as you could get, but PIRA would always come up with a method of attacking it.

After a brief walk round the cab, Dave was back in his seat now and strapping in. I completed the before take-off checks.

'OK Let's go. Let's go,' he said.

'Roger that.'

We had been on the ground for four minutes.

'Red One Fifty, Gazelle lifting departing to the north, Red One Fifty.' Lifting into the hover, I pushed on the right pedal and turned on the spot through 90 degrees to my right so I could check behind the aircraft through my right window.

I was pushing against power. The Fenestron tail rotor at the rear comprising 13 light alloy blades shrouded in the tailfin was a miracle of engineering and unique to the Gazelle helicopter. Rotating at 5,800rpm, it prevented the whole body of the fuselage from spinning in the opposite direction to the main rotor above. Turning over

10 times faster than the main rotor and with the lever effect of being on the end of a long tube at the rear of the aircraft, it could also be used to manoeuvre the aircraft as I was doing now.

By increasing the angle of all 13 blades, the tail was being pulled to the left against the rotation of the main rotor thereby allowing the nose of the helicopter to rotate to the right. The oil level in the tail rotor gearbox was one thing you checked before every flight!

The bottom of the cloud was now only 500ft above us scudding along in a fresh south-westerly breeze. We were going to have to continue this sortie low level.

Having checked behind and as I turned straight again, I pulled the collective and lifted allowing the rotation to continue until I faced northwest, pulled up over the fence skirted the terraced houses opposite the base and flew away gaining 50 knots rapidly now without the extra weight in the back. Spots of light rain appeared on the canopy. Having followed me on the controls, Dave now turned his attention to the complex task of low-level navigation and map folding his way across the terrain. The rules to avoid detection over an area where the specific threat location was unknown, such as South Armagh, were fairly common sense. Vary airspeed, height, and course and when crossing unavoidable ridgelines, select the *lowest* crossing point and then fly quickly down the other side to avoid too much exposure. We were also taught to fly along the edge of a wood or vegetation below the tree height rather than over it and how to negotiate large electricity transmission lines by gingerly flying under them. It required constant practice hence the fact that much of UK was designated a Low Flying Area.

'Right, we will go back via the watchtowers. That way, we will be under constant visual from the guys manning them and you get to see where they are.'

It was only my first week of my tour here and I was getting to know the lie of the land. I nodded back. Sounds like a good plan to me.

It was soon to be disrupted though.

Our first waypoint was Golf Two Zero, the watchtower on the border at Drummuckavall. Stood on a 300ft hill it was named after the Irish *Dromach a'Bhafal* or 'ridge of the great dyke'. There was a border crossing here which could be kept under continual observation and before the permanent structure was completed, had been the scene of an IRA ambush in the 1970s when three Fusiliers tragically lost their lives manning a covert OP.

I banked sharp right around the town and headed southeast at tree top height. The border here was less than two miles away and one of the closest crossing points to Crossmaglen. We skirted close to the north of the tower, its scaffolding and communication aerials providing a stark contrast to the emerald, green countryside.

Bandit Country all right.

Next, due east zero nine zero degrees on the magnetic compass and again just over two miles away stood Golf Three Zero at Glassdrumman. Neatly tucked into an enclave into the Irish Republic, this tower had been specifically sited to overlook another notorious crossing point at Ballybinaby. Named after the Irish *An Ghlasdrommaain* or 'the green ridge', it had been mortared countless times and could accommodate 32 men underground.

Events were about to get a little more interesting.

On Flight Safety Common…

'Gazelle Four this is Lynx Three can you call battalion ops on Channel Twelve.'

Dave switched channels on the secure VHF and called in to Bessbrook.

'Gazelle Four, would you like a task?'

'Ready copy Gazelle Four.'

'Golf Four Zero has had a sighting of an abandoned vehicle across the road leading into Forkill belonging to known PIRA at Grid 010615. Driver appears to be slumped against steering wheel. Lynx Three is unable to check it 'cos low on fuel. Ready to copy vehicle?'

'Go ahead Buzzard.'

'Vehicle is a red Ford Mondeo registration MIB7004.'

'Copy that we will go and have a closer look.'

Dave turned sideways and pointed at the Doppler navaid in the console between us. 'Right let's just slow up and orbit here until I get a fix on this thing.'

Reaching down with his right hand while I banked right, he selected a blank waypoint number, eight or nine were usually spare and then with WP-GRID already set, he set both adjacent toggle switches to slew UP. This reset the display to read our present six figure map coordinates. By slewing up or down first with the left toggle switch for eastings and then the right toggle for northings, the numbers could be adjusted to the required coordinates.

With the map reference entered into the computer all I had to do was glance down to the box and if the horizontal warning bars were illuminating left, turn the cab left until the warning bars extinguished one by one until they were all out. We were then on track directly to that point. Simple but brilliant technology and I loved it.

However, things were about to become a lot more difficult.

# 2

# Spinning Up

## Tidworth, April 1987

I am sitting behind my desk in the squadron office shuffling paper. I am 28 years old; a captain in the Royal Engineers and I am bored and somewhat disillusioned with the Army. I have given a lot of thought to leaving but cannot bring myself to take any action. Although I have had a decent enough time so far, postings to Germany, tours in Northern Ireland, Falkland Islands and an exercise in Kenya, things are getting stale, and I am resigned to more staff work as I grind up the promotion ladder.

But then a glossy pamphlet arrived on my desk that would change my life. It was called New Horizons or something like that. Produced by the Director of Manning (Army) and featuring a picture of a cheerful looking officer on the front, I opened it up.

The Army was currently suffering a high wastage of junior officers who were not converting to Regular service after their eight-year short service period was up or were leaving for other reasons. Designed to incentivise and retain this valuable manpower, the publication was in four short sections outlining opportunities outside 'normal' regimental service for tours up to three years in duration.

The first part described becoming attached to the Parachute Brigade by undertaking the airborne selection course at Aldershot. Maroon beret.

Definitely not for me, I wasn't the Para type and nowhere near physically fit enough…I moved on. The next section was Commando training! Great for an infanteer, I thought, but crawling around in the mud down at Plymouth with the Royal Marines had lost its appeal.

Thirdly, it introduced the Special Forces, The SAS. Nice idea but a non-starter. The failure rate was brutal, and the preparation would take months.

The last section was about the Army Air Corps (AAC) and a thing called CREST.

I read on with growing interest.

Since 1986, the AAC had been restructuring their aircrew manning. They were transitioning from Pilot and Aircrewman/Observer per aircraft to two Pilots per aircraft. CREST stood for Crew RESTructuring effectively doubling the need for pilots. I had envied colleagues in the past who had somehow got commissions in the AAC direct from Sandhurst, but it was an incredibly small part of the Army in those days and incredibly difficult to get in.

Hang on this could be it! I had never lost my love of flying but had always been thwarted in any attempt to become a pilot. I had been in the Air Cadets at school and had even had a few goes on a Chipmunk about 10 years ago. That's what they used for training and also part of the selection process. This was it; I was going to go for it, come what may, this was my chance, a fantastic opportunity…

Until I read the requirements. *Maximum age thirty years*. Crikey I was nearly 29 now. Clutching the pamphlet, I went into the Chief Clerk's domain and asked him for the relevant application form for flying training.

He chuckled, 'Who's this for now then? I've had a Biggles a week come into the office since this came out!'. 'Actually, it's for me Chief, I am going to give it a shot.' He grinned and then proceeded to tell me about all the sergeant pilots he knew who had applied and failed at some stage of the application or training or how he knew this, that, and the other thing about the Air Corps.

'Just let me have the form Chief please'

The regimental second-in-command admitted to me that he had once 'wrestled with the Gazelle' as he put it… and lost.

Would I also fall flat on my face and fail at this?

There was one more hurdle. The form required my Commanding Officer's signature.

Anyway, honest to God that's how it started and once I had convinced my CO that my motivation was to become the first Royal Engineer officer pilot in a long time and he had warned me of the long-term career consequences, for which quite frankly, I couldn't give a damn, I was set on the journey.

Spring turned to beautiful summer, and I was cycling into the barracks from my married quarter home when I passed our Chief Clerk on the way…

'Bloody Hell Sir, you will have to cycle faster than that to get airborne! I think your papers have arrived.'

Speeding up, I swung into the squadron office and there was my little brown envelope marked 'Officers and Aircrew Selection Centre, RAF Biggin Hill.' The Royal Air Force were responsible for aircrew selection across all three branches of the Services and you either passed their aptitude tests or failed. There was no middle ground, no second chance, no appeal, just *Suitable* or *Not Suitable*. My appointment was in just two weeks' time.

After some preparation involving an Amstrad computer and a game called 'Apache,' I amazed myself by passing various aptitude tests, an all day long medical, an ECG and EEG, and some physical tests including measurement of arms, legs, head size etcetera and the next stage was to report to Middle Wallop for Flying Grading. As part of the selection process, and to weed out the guys with bad attitude under instruction, they wanted to see what you were like in an aircraft. Consisting of 12 one-hour flying lessons in a Chipmunk aeroplane trainer and a test at the end, it was almost half a Private Pilots Course but without the solo flying element. Instructors would be changed halfway through for fair treatment throughout. The pass rate was low however and there was very little if any feedback. Still, even if you failed you had 13 free flying hours in a logbook, so it was a great gig.

Middle Wallop, situated five miles west of Andover, is a Second World War airfield famous for being active during the Battle of Britain in 1940. Originally meant for Bomber Command, five large C-type hangers and a control tower were built but the runways were all grass. It then become home to a flying training school before squadrons of Spitfires and Hurricanes moved in and it became a fighter station. It was not until 1957 that it became a School of Army Aviation although there had been some experimental helicopter flying there before that.

Everyone wore the light blue beret and the whole place had a different feel and attitude to a Royal Engineer regiment. Way more relaxed and with plenty of civilians employed, it was a breath of fresh air compared to Tidworth.

I am told the three ingredients of a successful flying career are aptitude, attitude... and well of course altitude!

I was determined to develop all three but first I would have to reacquaint myself with the de Havilland Chipmunk or 'Chippie'.

> The Chipmunk Mark 10 is designed as a basic trainer aircraft and has a fixed undercarriage, fully castoring tailwheel, and totally enclosed tandem cockpits. With full dual control, the leading edges of the wings and tail plane and the fuselage are metal covered. The remainder of the wings and the control services are fabric covered. The aircraft is powered by a Gypsy Major Mark 8 engine driving a fixed pitch metal propeller and is fitted with a self-indexing cartridge starter. When flown solo, the pilot should occupy the front cockpit.
>
> Pilots Notes A.P. 308a

Oh, those early summer days between 23 May and 30 June 1988!

Nearly an entire year had passed after the Commandant had said those words that were to set me on the path to glory: 'Yes, Peter I think we can train you to fly the Gazelle.'

Learning to fly is not inherently difficult, you can train a monkey to fly so they say, but not everyone can do it, especially in a given time frame and a fixed budget. It also requires 100 percent dedication and concentration.

I was back at Wallop and eager to start the Army Pilots Course.

It was good to see the 'old and bold' team of fixed wing instructors were still there. All civilians, they had a diverse mixture of backgrounds, and all had been military pilots of one form or other. My instructor was 'Ben' Gunn. We used to fly two or three lessons a day depending on the weather. Weaving from side to side across the grass airfield to clear the view in front of the cockpit, we did endless circuits until he finally cleared me solo after six and a half hours on the 1st of June, a month before my 30th birthday!

The rest of the course consisted of two other officers – Sean, from the Royal Army Ordnance Corps (RAOC), Ian from the 7th Duke of Edinburgh's Gurkha Rifles who already had a Private Pilot's Licence – and five Senior Non-Commissioned Officers from the Army Air Corps who were all Lynx or Gazelle aircrewmen observers. To provide humour and elan to the course there were two Royal Marines corporals, also aircrewmen observers.

Once solo we completed loads of navigation flights both dual and solo, an introduction to instrument flying, and a few aerobatics culminating in a Final Handling Test which you had to pass, or you went home. No second chance at that late stage. The nerves were excruciating.

The horror: to get all the way through and fail the FHT!

After three weeks leave and told to forget everything about flying, I was back to start 'wrestling with the Gazelle,' otherwise known as Basic Rotary. Exercise Eight was learning to hover. My instructor, a retired naval aviator called Mr Collins, took me through the ground briefing and then the air exercise. The hover is a basic requirement in helicopter flying since it is the prerequisite to safe landings. The good book states '…a large area should be selected without any obstructions.' Well two football fields should be enough, but luckily, we had that at Wallop, acre upon acre of beautifully mown grass airfield to practice in.

Imagine you are sat with the cyclic stick in your right hand, the collective lever in your left hand and feet on both pedals. After trying each one in turn, you are given all three together. Focussing on a tree 75 to 100 metres away and into wind, the machine starts to drift to the right. You sense it and move your right hand a little to the left to compensate. But then something else happens. By tilting the disc, you have lost a small amount of upwards force, so you raise the collective slightly with your left hand to prevent the machine sinking to the ground. But then something else happens. By raising the collective, you have demanded more power and the nose of the machine yaws to the left with the torque reaction so you must apply right pedal to keep facing your tree… but then the wind gusts and you start moving backwards slightly.

Now you are accelerating to the left, you have overcompensated with the lever and the machine wants to leap upwards away from the ground, spinning the nose to the left even more… and you are starting to travel backwards so you move the cyclic forwards, and guess what happens? You start sinking again but you have already lowered the lever to prevent the helicopter leaping airborne so now you are about to hit the ground with the nose spinning right this time… all in less time than it has taken for you to read this!

'I have control' says your instructor patiently.

After about 20 minutes of these gyrations and soaked in sweat, you return to the hangar ever humbled. Next time out, just when you think I am never going to get this, you do and you hover, really hover safely for the first time. Remember this moment for it will stay with you forever. The brain will never let you forget how to do it now, much like riding a bicycle.

You are hooked!

I had just bought a ridiculously small cottage in a pretty village about five miles away and we were busy during the summer decorating. At night I lay in bed listening to helicopters night flying from Wallop. You could never really escape the sound although our village was a no-fly zone due to the number of stables and paddocks around.

I remember reading somewhere when flying was in its infancy that early aviators in the Royal Flying Corps were recruited from cavalry regiments because they demonstrated ability in controlling a horse!

Basic Rotary ended at the end of October with another Final Handling Test.

Now followed the 'real' flying, 70 hours of instruction from Army Air Corps instructors on operational flying techniques such as advanced low-level map reading, artillery fire observation and controlling, underslung loads, endless enemy fighting vehicle recognition classes and more demanding instrument flying.

The highlight was probably mountain flying in Snowdonia. Once you have landed on the top of Snowden at 3,500ft, taking the train up to the summit will never be the same again!

Eventually the Final Handling Test with the Chief Flying Instructor and then the excitement of the Wings Parade in our draughty hangar in front of friends and family where we are awarded our Army Flying Badge or 'wings,' a simple crown surmounted by a golden lion with white wings on a black background. Those stressful months are over now, never really sure if you are going to make it to the end, but you do, and you qualify as an Army pilot, the single best thing that eclipses your life to date.

But where to be posted and which machine? I had expressed a preference to remain in the UK – as I had just bought a house nearby rather than any operational considerations – and I also was indifferent about the choice of helicopter, whether to stay on Gazelle or undergo more jeopardy by remaining at Wallop for a Lynx Conversion Course and an almost certain posting to BAOR. The appeal of flying a bigger faster weapon-mounted helicopter was still there, so I left it to fate. In the end, Sean got his Lynx preference, and I got mine, whereas Ian went to a Gazelle squadron at Detmold.

I was to report to Airfield Camp, Netheravon on Salisbury Plain!

To a Royal Engineer interested in aviation history this was an interesting place to be as this grassy site situated on the plain to the east of the River Avon was an original Royal Flying Corps aerodrome. Formerly a calvary school, Netheravon became an extension of the Central Flying School at Upavon just a few kilometres north and then after the first few months of the war became a base for the formation of new squadrons of the RFC. The Officers Mess had carved RFC wings over the entrance which still remain today, and it was here at this austere establishment that I reported to 658 Squadron, 7 Regiment, Army Air Corps on a cold crisp winter's day in February 1989.

# 3

# Croslieve

The weather was becoming an issue now, the watchtower on the top of Croslieve Mountain was definitely in cloud as was the Romeo tower on the opposite side of Forkill. Both OPs overlooked the small town and the border area just a short distance away. We reminded ourselves of our obligations to Military Flying Regulations which clearly stated the minimum weather criteria for visual flying. Nowhere near as prohibitive as civilian air traffic rules, the Regs allowed us to 'maintain forward visibility of one kilometre and visual contact or sight of the ground.' The cloud base must not be less than 300ft above ground or water level.

Such conditions were hazardous with obstacles around and would inevitably lead to reducing speed to give yourself more time to adjust to the picture.

We weren't in those conditions yet however and with both watchtowers in the mist, our Gazelle was the only means of confirming this report, so we continued.

We turned north away from Forkill and picked up a small lane running to the east of the mountain. I flew slowly down the right side of the road so Dave in the left seat as observer could get a better view down the lane itself. A small country lane with scattered housing and farm buildings, there were no vehicles to be seen anywhere. The digits on the Doppler box were flashing now indicating we had reached the waypoint that had been entered. If the coordinates were correct, the car would be in a 100-metre size box from our position.

Sometimes you get the notion that things aren't quite right, and I started to feel uneasy.

Only a month ago, before I arrived in the province, the East Tyrone Brigade of the IRA had brought down Gazelle ZB687 flown by a single AAC pilot and carrying three soldiers of the King's Own Scottish Border Regiment (KOSB). They had been providing support for a joint RUC/Army patrol investigating suspicious vehicle activity at a border crossing point near Clogher in County Tyrone. Scouting ahead, the Gazelle would have been used to alert the guys on the ground to potential ambush sites, suspect vehicles, or possible Improvised Explosive Devices.

Sound familiar?

On this occasion, however the helicopter itself was the target, the alert at the border crossing almost certainly a decoy intended to lure the Gazelle into an ambush. At around 1630 hours – just before dusk – a five-man Active Service Unit opened fire with a General Purpose Machine Gun and AK-47s. One round is all it took, fracturing an engine oil pipe leading to a low-level engine failure. The helicopter crashed in a field near the border and luckily, they all survived but the Gazelle was a complete write-off.

I certainly felt we were in a potentially similar situation with the added disadvantage of no back-up ground patrols.

'Eyes on target,' Dave had spotted the vehicle ahead; a red car sideways on blocking the road ahead. I slowed to hover in a field about 250 metres short. We were extremely vulnerable here but there was some cover from the high ground from a small industrial warehouse on our left.

Was my Aircraft Commander thinking the same thing?

Luckily today we were flying one of the pair of 'cabs' in the squadron which were still fitted with the GOA or Gazelle Observation Aid. A gyro-stabilised periscopic sight (meaning the image would remain steady) was mounted in the roof above the Aircraft Commander's head. Designed for another war on the battlefield of North-West Europe, its purpose was to identify and report on enemy tanks and armoured vehicles. We were over a different 'battlefield' now but it would prove to be extremely useful. 'Soldiers first, pilots second.'

Reaching above his head, Dave swung the short downtube into a vertical mode and adjusted the eyepiece to suit his eye position.

'Right hold it steady'

Dave switched the power switch to on, and selected high magnification, and then using a small thumbstick on the control box sighted the vehicle.

'Eyes on target'

'Roger that'

'Wait, there are two vehicles I think'

Behind and slightly to the left from our position another vehicle was in a ditch on the left-hand side of the road where it made a sharp 90-degree bend to the right running east. For all intents and purposes, it looked like a traffic accident, but was it?

Three things that we noticed probably saved our lives.

One – there was no damage apparent to either vehicle.

Two – the 'driver' in the red car didn't look real. There was something about the size and posture. Most unconscious bodies slump to one side due to the weight of the head but here, the 'driver' appeared to be propped up by something behind him or her.

Three – it was deserted. Not a soul in sight. Normally people would have heard a crash or screeching of tyres and rushed out to help. But this definitely wasn't normal…

That was enough for me.

'It's a f***ing dummy!'

Cleverly positioned in the front vehicle, the 'driver' was a dummy slumped against the steering wheel. It was obviously a come-on designed to lure Security Forces to the scene so that some unspeakable act of violence could be committed.

I turned us on the spot and retraced our flight path back to Forkill. Dave reported on the Tac VHF secure while I concentrated on the flying. The workload was high now and concentration was intense. I orbited slowly and reassured myself that if the 'bad guys' had planned a helicopter shoot it would probably have happened by now.

Was the cover from the industrial building the thing? Advancing any closer would have left us totally exposed from the high ground to the left. We couldn't know.

FLY THE AIRCRAFT!

We had done all we could. No one was at risk here. It looked to me as if it had been set up as a road traffic accident with a Command Wire IED (Improvised Explosive Device) in one of the vehicles – probably the one in the ditch – or as a possible killing zone for a shoot at whoever attended the scene.

Heading north-east now towards Newry, visibility about 3 miles in the 'clag' as we used to say. I glanced at the fuel contents gauge. It was indicating 200 kilograms, just over half full (fuel is read by weight not content in aircraft). At a normal consumption of two kilos per minute and subtracting the 40 kilograms minimum fuel requirement by law, we had 80 minutes of flying time left.

Dave selected Waypoint One to give a bearing a distance to RAF Aldergrove Airport, our squadron home base. Blinking, it read back '010 degrees 30 nautical miles.' Fifteen minutes and we could be home. There was just one problem.

We could hardly see anything.

The wipers sweeping backwards and forwards across the plexiglass canopy were very distracting. There were plenty of high and low electricity pylons and wires between 100ft and 300ft on the way back. It made sense to go back at high level and we both agreed that a radar approach would be the best option.

# 4

# RAF Aldergrove

*Then down through the fleecy clouds below,*
*The FE drifted fast:*
*The observer thought of his future,*
*And the pilot thought of his past…*

The Wreck of the Old FE
WW1 RFC Song

Approaching the city of Newry from the south, the weather started to 'improve' allowing us to gain a bit of height. Away to the right, the brooding but beautiful outline of the Mourne Mountains was now visible on the far side of Carlingford Lough. Ten years ago, I had enjoyed a walking weekend with a colleague, and we had camped out in the middle of nowhere. County Down was considered 'safe' to resident troops and the local population but increasingly there were news reports of some activity in the area mainly directed towards the brave men and women of the Ulster Defence Regiment.

'I have control Sir, can you give Aldergrove a call'

I relinquished control to my colleague and grabbed my trusty Ops chart. Swapping duties, I would be managing the radios and the navigation while Dave got a bit of flying in.

Using our civilian callsign ARMY AIR 328, I called Aldergrove Radar.

'ALDERGROVE RADAR, ARMY AIR 328, GAZELLE, ONE MILE WEST OF NEWRY, HEADING 010 DEGREES AT 800FT AMSL, 2 PERSONS ON BOARD REQUESTING CLIMB AND RADAR ADVISORY AND RECOVER TO ALDERGROVE.'

'ARMY AIR 328, ALDERGROVE RADAR ROGER MAINTAIN HEADING AND SQUAWK 4367.'

I reached down to the PTR 446 Identification Friend or Foe set and dialled in the number. The set would now be transmitting coded pulse replies in answer to interrogation signals transmitted by the secondary surveillance radar at RAF

Aldergrove. Although an operational RAF station and home to 72 Squadron, it was also Belfast International where passenger jets were arriving and departing daily. We didn't want to hit one of those on our way back!

'ARMY AIR 328, ALDERGROVE RADAR, YOU ARE IDENTIFIED TWO MILES NORTHEAST OF NEWRY, CLIMB 2,500FT ON ALTIMETER 994 HECTOPASCALS and TURN LEFT HEADING 355 DEGREES.'

Excellent, we could now climb away into the cloud above knowing they would keep us clear of anything else flying around in the vicinity.

I gave out an 'Ops Normal' call to Squadron Ops on the Tac FM giving our Estimated Time of Arrival and a safety call on the UHF Common stating our intentions to climb, just in case. Glancing at the Outside Air Temperature gauge, it read five degrees Celsius. Flying was not permitted in icing conditions and for the purposes of standardisation, this was defined as cloud or fog within the temperature range of zero degrees to minus 30 degrees when the visibility is less than 1,000 metres.

It was vital for us both to monitor this little instrument now as the temperature would reduce rapidly once in the cloud. We could expect a drop of at least two degrees per 1,000ft of altitude.

By now Dave was concentrating fully on the instruments in front of him. Flying in cloud is only possible because of the presence of an amazing instrument called the attitude indicator which took pride of place at the top of the panel.

Without this 'artificial horizon' it would be quite easy to lose control of the aircraft rapidly. The gyroscopic ball was coloured light grey and black with the line between them representing 'wings level'.

The ball was free to rotate up and down and bank left and right in front of a fixed aircraft symbol. All you had to do was keep the sodding thing on the white line between the grey part and the black part and you would be flying level all right but what about straight?

If the ball tilted so that the white line was running for example diagonally slightly from bottom left to top right, you were in a turn to the right and would continue to turn until you made the sodding thing line up again with the white line.

Yes, the concentration was mind-blowing but fun and any little deviation soon became second nature to correct. By scanning from this central instrument out to the compass and then the airspeed and then altimeter and vertical speed indicator, each time returning to the 'horizon,' you would be able to keep complete control.

No autopilot for us Army soldier pilots. I believe the Royal Air Force and Royal Navy Gazelles were fitted with one.

As we climbed and levelled at 2,500ft on the altimeter, South Armagh seemed far away. We were in a different world, a civilian managed airspace rather than a military operational zone all in a few minutes.

One degree Celsius said the temperature.

'If it gets any colder ask for descent to 2,000ft.' Dave had already noticed.
Sharp, I thought.

The upper surfaces of the laminated glass fibre rotor blades would start to gather ice making them heavier and the extra drag would start to slow them down stressing the gearbox and ultimately the engine. By descending back into 'warmer' air, we could prevent the Gazelle icing up and vibrating itself to pieces.

I sat monitoring the instrument panel and the radio thinking of how versatile this amazing machine was. No other aircraft that I know of could one minute be hovering in a field at 8ft and the next minute become a pseudo airliner awaiting vectoring into an international airport along with Boeing 737s or 757s.

Aldergrove Radar: 'WHAT TYPE OF APPROACH WOULD YOU LIKE SIR?'

'A good one' joked Dave on the intercom.

'REQUESTING SRA TO RUNWAY 25, MINIMUMS 920FT, REQUEST LATEST WEATHER.'

Decisive moment.

Was the cloud base high enough for us to see the ground by the time we reached our minimum descent altitude?

The rationale behind a surveillance radar approach is that it allows an aircraft to descend below a safety altitude in instrument meteorological conditions (IMC) and conduct an approach following a set of laid-down control procedures. This ensures that descent below safety altitude is safe and the risk to life associated with controlled flight into terrain is minimised. I stress the word minimised. Not eradicated!

The radar approaches would terminate at two miles from the airport. By that distance, we had to be able to see the ground or we would have to climb away back into the cloud and try again, resulting in a very high workload.

The cloud base had now lifted to about 1,000 feet in the Belfast area so seeing the ground should not be a problem but shortly something else would liven up an already knackering day's flying.

RAF Aldergrove was home to 665 Squadron Army Air Corps and 72 Squadron Royal Air Force on the south side of the main runway. Occupying two main hangars on the north side was the civilian airport terminal and the private flying club and other buildings. The squadron had about 10 Gazelles and eight Lynx helicopters during the time I was there. Two of the Gazelles were allocated to 'G' flight for 'special recce duties.' 'I cannot tell you what I do because then I would have to kill you afterwards' was the standard response to any inquisition.

We had about 20 aircraft commanders and 12 pilots commanded by a major, with each flight managed by a captain flight commander, usually the most senior in terms of flying hours. I had only been in the province for less than three weeks, and although a qualified Gazelle Aircraft Commander myself back on the mainland, I had not yet had my in-theatre check to get me to that status here.

We would commence our descent from seven miles at 2,500ft. The radar controller gave us headings to line up with the runway and we did our final landing checks.

'DESCEND NOW TO MAINTAIN A THREE DEGREE GLIDEPATH.'

Dave lowered the collective slightly and the vertical speed indicator registered a descent of 500ft per minute, our forward speed of 100 knots remained constant.

'FIVE MILES FROM TOUCHDOWN, ON CENTRELINE, ON GLIDEPATH.'

Dave was doing an excellent job in the left seat but then things started to go wrong. ALTERNATOR caption on the warning panel.

At the same time, the little green and yellow stripey flag flicked across the 'artificial horizon' effectively saying 'Don't use this anymore!'.

Great I thought, it only had to last another couple of minutes. I pressed the RESET button, but the flag wouldn't budge.

'Better use the standby' I said as I flicked the alternator switch to OFF.

Dave was already on it squinting at the small standby horizon on his side of the main instrument panel. Identical to the main failed instrument, it took its power from the 12v DC system through a static inverter which converted the DC to AC power needed to keep the gyro spinning inside.

The Emergency Checklist stated the bleeding obvious 'land as soon as practicable.'

'FOUR MILES FROM TOUCHDOWN, ON CENTRELINE, SLIGHTLY HIGH, INCREASE RATE OF DESCENT.'

We could see the ground coming into view now and the eerie grey, white world became green and yellow and blue again.

Continuing down the imaginary slope, we were approaching the minimum height above the ground that was legal without visual contact.

'APPROACHING MDH, RADAR APPROACH TERMINATED, WHEN VISUAL CONTACT TOWER ONE ONE EIGHT DECIMAL THREE.'

I read back the frequency while Dave held the cab level at this safe height about two miles from the beginning of the runway and ran in towards the field.

Parking up on her designated spot outside the squadron hangar, Dave reached up and pulled the yellow throttle lever fully aft and gated it, so it was secure. The engine wound down to a mere 25,500rpm and the rotors began to slow. Once below 170rpm the rotor brake could be applied to speed up the process of stopping the rotation. After one minute, putting the START switch to off silenced the Astazou engine, and I eased myself outside to walk around the Gazelle looking for any damage, oil and fuel leaks. All good.

Walking back to the hangar in silence, we were both drained and exhausted. While Dave went to sign the cab in with the REME technicians, I went to the armoury to hand in my weapons and ammunition.

Nobody was in the crew room, so I walked across the large hangar.

The hangar had a distinctive oily smell, but the floor was absolutely spotless. Parked here and there were two or three of both Lynx and Gazelle in various degrees of dismantlement with covers off, rotors missing and even engines removed.

The engineers would work through the night on these machines, and it was quite likely that they would be flying sorties as early as tomorrow. The Light Aircraft Detachment or LAD provided daily servicing keeping the right number of cabs available to meet the requirements of the flying programme.

On average a 25-hour check would take as little as an hour or two, while 21 days were needed for a major 800-hour service on a Gazelle. It was great to chat to the guys but there was a dividing line. Once inside the hangar the cabs were 'theirs' and it was customary to ask permission to visit a particular cab undergoing maintenance. The number of operational flying hours were of course recorded by somebody, and I learnt that during the previous year, the Northern Ireland Regiment's 17 Gazelles (which included 655 Squadron and City Flight) had flown 8,652 hours.

The squadron shuttle bus was waiting in its usual spot, and I stepped on board for the 20-minute ride back to Alexander Barracks where the mess accommodation, offices and domestic side of life was located. I enjoyed the bus ride. It gave you a few moments to unwind and take you to a different quieter almost normal environment. Already on the bus sitting waiting to leave was Captain Isobel Harding, or 'Izzie' as she liked to be called by fellow officers.

I sat down next to her on the all-but-empty bus.

'Hi Izzie, unusual to see you here!' I said, 'What are you up to?'

'Just been delivering some reports to the office, have to be delivered by hand you see, Confidential reports and stuff like that.' I had met her before briefly in the Officers Mess. She had dark black hair and her emerald eyes glinted back at me. Izzie was the attractive regimental Assistant Adjutant, one of the roles for WRAC officers in those days before women were fully integrated into the Army. There were no female pilots in those days. Extremely popular, not least because she was the only female living in the Officers Mess, she was on a two-year posting to Northern Ireland. You only really saw her in the mess at breakfast or in the bar, so it was unusual to see her in full uniform or 'battle gear.'

*Killer* by Adamski was playing on the bus radio.

'How did it go today?'

I related our sortie and the incident with the supposed car accident.

Her eyes grew wider 'So that was you!' She smiled. 'Hey that's all kicked off. I saw the reports they called out FELIX from Bessbrook and two armoured RUC patrols are down there.' FELIX was the codeword for the Ammunition Technical Officer from the Royal Army Ordnance Corps whose unenviable job was to make the area safe and neutralise the device.

'The CO saw the INT Report and he wants a report first thing tomorrow!'

I slumped. All I wanted was a beer and a shower not to sit down and draft a bloody report after the day we had.

She saw my reaction, 'Only joking' she laughed.

'Hey a few of us are going out tonight for a drink after work, I've got the crappy car again.'

The permanent members of the Northern Ireland Regiment and the squadron were able to live in married quarters at Aldergrove. It was only the single officers and men who lived in the various messes. The Army had, and still has, a trilogy of divisions between Officers, Warrant Officers and Sergeants and Junior Ranks. Some barracks had a Corporals Mess as well, making four divisions of messing arrangements. Highly inefficient in economic terms but important for maintaining discipline.

Our target for the night was the Dunadry Inn, a few miles from the base and considered a safe place to visit. County Antrim was largely Protestant and few terrorist-related incidents took place here. Sitting around a table with a band of brothers, I felt this was the best place in the world to be at the moment.

I winked at Izzie. She had driven the 'crappy' staff car with local plates that she had the use of as a matter of course in her job. She was always going on about her 'boyfriend in Cornwall' to shake us off but we knew he didn't exist. Who could blame her? Most of the single guys on roulement tours like myself had someone back on the mainland hoping, or not, that they came back at the end of four months tour of duty. I was not due to fly until tomorrow evening, a training flight with the Major that would introduce me to flying with night vision goggles. With the laughter and noise, I drifted away into normality again.

# 5

# Shackleton Shadows

I am walking out from the floodlit squadron hangar at Aldergrove towards Gazelle ZB670 with Major Sam Duncan, the 665 Squadron OC, to complete my introduction to flying with Night Vision Goggles or NVG. All pilots had to complete approximately 5 hours of training before being released to operate on the line with other qualified NVG pilots.

Besides being the OC, Sam was a Qualified Helicopter Instructor (QHI) and a legend in the Corps. During the Falklands War in 1982, he had been awarded the Distinguished Flying Cross for repeatedly flying his Scout helicopter under fire to rescue wounded soldiers from the Scots Guards during the attack on Mount Tumbledown.

A few months before my arrival he had taken part in another rescue from a mountainside, this time picking up an unconscious soldier who had slipped climbing with his patrol up to the Golf Four Zero watchtower at Croslieve. Now 'under fire from snow and ice' he had used NVG to manoeuvre his Lynx helicopter to reach the pick-up point and take the casualty back to Bessbrook Mill.

Once airborne, we departed to the east towards Belfast and Sam climbed to safe altitude before we started 'goggling.'

The emerald, green and grey surface of daytime was now a black and yellow landscape. The moon was partly full and illuminated the panorama around us. Yellow sodium clusters of towns and villages divided ink black open countryside while white ribbons of headlights indicated roads connecting them. Occasional isolated red lights marked security bases or towers. To the east, Belfast dominated the skyline with the massive black lump of Divis Mountain shielding part of the city. To the west, the shimmering expanse of Lough Neagh, the largest inland lake in the British Isles. Irish mythology tells how the lake was formed when Ireland's legendary giant Fionn mac Cumhaill (Finn McCool) scooped up a chunk of earth and tossed it at a Scottish rival. It fell into the Irish Sea, forming the Isle of Man, while the crater left behind filled with water to form Lough Neagh.

Flying at night often had an ethereal magic to it and I was going to get my fair share on this tour. Cecil Lewis, the First World War pilot describes night flying in his book *Sagittarius Rising*:

> …again a feeling of amazement gripped me, that I alone in a frail contrivance, should have been given such keys to the paths of heaven, should have found my way to this undreamed-of paradise of night: more marvellous, more serene, than any, earthly landscape under the garish blatancy of day.

Sam started off by pointing out the various modifications in the cockpit necessary to support NVG flying such as the lighting. Aircraft instruments are easier to read under higher levels of interior illumination, however, this need must be balanced with the ability to see outside and the hazard of interior lights reflecting off the Perspex windows. The moon is the primary source of natural light at night and sky glow is a term for the ambient light produced by the sun when below the horizon.

During normal night flying without googles the cockpit instruments are lit with a red light, reducing the glare and thereby making them easier to read. Red lighting enables you to keep your night vision for longer, but they are unsuitable for flying with goggles because along with normal white light can create intensely bright effects on the display whereas it was found that blue filters made them easier to view and interpret. Due to the lack of a clear horizon at night, much of night flying is effectively instrument flying even though you are not actually in cloud.

The Aviators Night Vision Imaging System (ANVIS) was a lightweight set of binoculars mounted on the helmet which could be swung down in front of your eyes in the forward position and locked. The goggles were powered by a battery attached to the rear of the helmet with Velcro pads and a short cable.

Night Vision Googles work by amplifying the existing ambient light energy to produce an enhanced display through the eyepiece in front of the eyes. The result of a complicated process of accelerating and multiplying electrons is a monochrome green image of the scene in front of you. Night becomes day as if someone had a giant green searchlight illuminating the ground and objects normally completely invisible in the dark are outlined in an eerie glow.

'Ok just try straight and level to begin with and then try a few turns,' Sam suggested. I clicked the goggles into position, adjusted the focus and eye position and peered into a different world.

Sam described the limitations which were immediately apparent, the horizontal field of view provided by the image intensifier tubes is only 40 degrees compared to the natural eye which is 200 degrees. You get no peripheral vision whatsoever and I had to get used to swinging my head from side to side to monitor the instruments and the view outside.

The vision generated was monocular, meaning reduced depth perception and distance estimation. The binocular vision that we have normally occurs due to the slightly different point of view between the right and left eye. This allows you to detect movement rates or relative motion as during movement, objects that are near to you appear to move towards you more quickly, while objects further away appear to move much more slowly.

This would become super important during the hover and landing manoeuvres where everything depended on relative motion.

Returning to base, Sam demonstrated an approach and landing under NVG although there was plenty of airfield lighting to assist, but I got a feel for what was to come in further instruction the following night.

The next evening, I was rostered with John, the squadron QHI, to continue the training where Major Sam had left off.

Our destination was Ballykelly Airfield *Whisky One Zero Five*, five miles east of Londonderry, a former RAF airfield and now home to 655 Squadron and an Army resident battalion, presently The Gloucestershire Regiment. Apart from the experience I would gain in flying to a different airfield, Ballykelly Airfield was not used for regular civil flying and therefore the large area of disused runways could be used for training purposes unlike busy Aldergrove. The aim was to fly some circuits all using NVG.

John was a no-nonsense type of guy, ex-Parachute Regiment. He never seemed particularly happy with anybody's flying but his bark was usually worse than his bite. However, you were always at the mercy of these types of guys who could bring an end to your flying career with a swipe of a pen if they took a dislike to you.

The way to survive was to agree with everything and never argue, remember 'Aptitude, Attitude and of course Altitude!'

Departing to the north-west over the lough on a cloudless moonlit night, the instructor demonstrated a zoom climb up to 2,500ft. Smoking along at 50ft and 120 knots, John pulled back the cyclic smoothly but firmly, trading speed for height and the Gazelle launched skywards just until we needed to level out, whereupon he pushed the nose down and accelerated back to 120 knots in the cruise. It was impressive if a little cowboy-like, but he liked to show off, I guess.

Halfway to Ballykelly we passed close to the Sperrin Mountains that lie in the west of Ulster. The highest peak here rises to 2,224ft, but on our track we flew to the east over Cartogher just 1,000ft below, towering over the Glenshane Pass which housed the main A6 Belfast/Londonderry Road.

John pointed out the codeword *Edgeware Road* to call on the Flight Safety Common frequency if using it as a low-level route through the mountains. The blackness of the Sperrins gave way to lower ground and the lights of Londonderry. There were actually three airfields here in close proximity: Londonderry (Eglington) which was home to a flying club, but later became City of Derry Airport; Limavady (another disused RAF airfield); and Ballykelly itself.

The important thing here was to identify the right one!

RAF Ballykelly opened in June 1941 as a base for RAF Coastal Command. In 1943 the main runway was extended and acquired an unusual characteristic in that it crosses an active railway line. Rules were put in place giving trains the right of way over landing aircraft. The base was used to conduct anti-submarine patrols and escort convoys over the Atlantic Ocean. At various times B-24 Liberator aircraft flew from Ballykelly in the fight against the U-boats, ranging from the Bay of Biscay to northern Norway. By the end of the war, Ballykelly-based squadrons had been responsible for sinking 12 U-boats, sharing with other aircraft and surface ships in the destruction of several others, and damaging many more.

A significant amount of the airfield site remains, including the three runways, some buildings also survived, including a post-war cantilever hangar specially created in the 1960s for the Shackletons – that became one of the biggest in the United Kingdom – and the control tower. The Avro Shackleton was a four-engine long range maritime patrol aircraft named after the famous polar explorer.

John pointed out that in daytime 'Just aim for the middle one', and at night the red light on a comms mast was clearly visible at Ballykelly, but I remember all three airfields looked remarkably the same from the air.

Wearing our NVG now, we made our approach to the centre of the airfield where the two main runways intersected. I started with the plain old hover. The image through the goggles was like black and white television, only the levels of grey that distinguish between dark and light colours were instead light and darker shades of green. Interpreting textures of objects is also an important visual clue that is missing, the difference between grass and tarmac for example.

I found it more difficult to detect drift, the cab moving sideways or forwards and backwards and that took a bit of getting used to.

To finish off our time at Ballykelly, flying up to 1,000ft above the airfield and warning everybody in the vicinity, John demonstrated the 'Nitesun' searchlight mounted on the port boom outside the fuselage. Switching the master switch on and pressing START for five seconds, initiated the arc and the ground lit up impressively. The beam width was about 10 degrees and could be adjusted from horizontal to 70 degrees down. The searchlight had an infrared filter on the front so it could be used in conjunction with other devices.

The aim was to search a selected area in a gently banked left-hand orbit in flood mode and then once a target had been acquired to use the spot mode. It was an impressive piece of equipment, but never used because it gave away your position beautifully of course, and almost became obsolete with the introduction of the Wescam thermal imaging cameras which were being introduced at that time. Mounted on the right skid of our Gazelle was a Brightstar infrared landing light. Specifically designed for use with helicopters, it was invisible to the naked eye when switched on so it could be used to illuminate a landing site when wearing NVG instead of the conventional white landing light.

Anyway, having convinced John that I could approach to a hover and then land on both grass and tarmac, we called in to Ballykelly Ops that we were finished, thanked them for using their airfield and departed.

John also pointed out the 'blooming effect.' Not a swear word but light blooming occurs when lights come into your field of view and a glow extends out from the source of light creating a sort of 'halo' effect.

Obeying the principle of always varying routes, we climbed out towards Derry and reached a safe altitude before flying over the city.

John wanted to point out *Whisky Seven Zero Five*, the helicopter landing site at Ebrington Barracks, home of the headquarters of 8 Infantry Brigade.[1]

From there, due south to Omagh in County Tyrone, codenamed *Yankee Zero One One* was Lisanelly Barracks, home to another resident battalion, a quick high-level orbit over the town and then we flew another 20 miles south-west to fly over Dungannon, codenamed *Yankee Four Five Three*. John took control and turned north back to Aldergrove.

'Gazelle Six Ops Normal ETA 10 minutes'

We had been airborne now for about one hour and a half, most of it on NVG and I was starting to feel the neck strain and fatigue due to the increased helmet weight of 1–2lbs and the head movement required to constantly scan backwards and forwards.

Shut down, weapons handed in, paperwork completed.

On the bus back to the barracks from the airfield, John was chatting to another pilot, and I had time to reflect on the situation. The Army had arrived in Ulster 1971 with guns and boots on the streets and was stoned and sniped at to begin with. Then came the Land Rovers along with 4-ton Bedford trucks which were attacked with stones and landmines, culvert bombs and mortars. The 'soft' vehicles were 'hardened' with Makralon GRP armour and slow armoured vehicles appeared in the province such as the Ferret Scout and the 1 Ton Humber wheeled personnel carrier – affectionately known as the 'Pig' – and the six-wheeled Saracen armoured personnel carrier, or 'Sarrican'.

These were met with even further bomb attacks and the decision was made to restrict all vehicle movement in hard Republican areas to prevent loss of life, so helicopters replaced them. Target replacing target replacing target.

---

1   A brigade is an army formation consisting of two or three battalions or regiments and commanded by a Brigadier

In escalating the assets, we had given the PIRA terrorist an interesting variety of materiel hardware to base their attacks on.

'The threat of machine gun attack against helicopters is real' Tom King the Secretary of State for Northern Ireland had admitted in the Commons in June 1989. He added 'a number of steps were taken some time ago to give all possible protection to helicopters in the important work that they do'. At least, the government were now coming to terms with the fact that the more assets you introduce the more targets you present to the terrorist and the situation just escalates.

Part of an amusing old RFC song from World War One reminded me of the frailty of our existence as pilots:

*Take the cylinder out of my kidneys,*
*The connecting rod out of my brain,*
*From the small of my back take the crankshaft,*
*And assemble the engine again…*

## 6

# Bad Guys Rule

## April 1990

One month later and I am now an Aircraft Commander, and to be briefed by the squadron intelligence officer on the latest state of play along with a few other newcomers to the team. Flight Lieutenant Bill Lord signed out the key from the Ops Room and opening a door marked "CONFIDENTIAL – No Entry." We entered the squadron intelligence room, and one wall was covered in a rogue's gallery of photographs of all the terrorists or 'players' known at that time to the Security Forces. This was all supposed to be shared information and it was Bill's job to keep it as up to date as possible.

Bill told us that PIRA had some 300 active Volunteers to call on, but these varied in role and numbers were difficult to agree on. Two years ago in 1988, it was claimed that they had no more than 30 experienced shooters and bombers north of the border formed into Active Service Units of four men each.

These ASUs were predominantly operating in the South Armagh Brigade, East and Mid Tyrone Brigades and Belfast with a few south of the border as well. The main players were all known to the intelligence community by name and address and in most cases, except South Armagh where information was scant, were under surveillance.

There were photographs of all the recent weapon finds and explosive types along with vehicles that had been used in attacks.

Bill now briefed us on the latest weapons situation, and it wasn't good.

Not for us that is, and things had definitely got more dangerous in the last couple of years,

'Well, you all know about the Ak-47 and the M60' started Bill 'there are a couple of new kids on the block now courtesy of Colonel Gadaffi.' Continuing, he said:

> 'The Libyan Colonel has long been a supporter of the IRA who he has claimed are liberating the Irish nation from the tyranny of British colonialism. There have been numerous shipments using fishing vessels and oil support vessels into the Republic which have found their way into Northern Ireland. Only some

20 percent of these consignments had been recovered. You need to read up on these weapons and learn their strengths and weaknesses so you can identify them if need be.'

I immediately thought that there wouldn't be much left of *me* to identify if they were used on my flimsy Gazelle.

Bill introduced the DShK 12.7mm 'Dushka' heavy machine gun which had become the Red Army's standard heavy machine gun after entering service in 1939 and remains in service today. Dushka means 'Sweetheart' and its half-inch round can penetrate 15mm thick armour at 500 metres and has an effective range of one kilometre.

> 'We think there are two of these somewhere in South Armagh and one, possibly two, in East Tyrone. Shoots will be being planned as we speak. Two years ago, Lynx XZ664 was brought down by 15 rounds close to Aughanduff Upper Mountain, five kilometres from Silverbridge and this was their first success with this weapon.'

Later I was told they may have been flying down a valley that had recently been put out of bounds.

> 'You will recognise it because of the slow rate of fire!'

PIRA would mount this beast on the back of a truck then uncover it and unleash hell. But it came with a price. It was too heavy to dismantle and carry away so it often would have to be sacrificed and left behind. It was hard to imagine that the young faces that stared down from the montage on the wall could be capable of such violence, but it was about to get worse.

It still requires considerable skill to hit a fast-moving object at low level with a machine gun vibrating wildly and by the time the round reaches the spot in the air that it was aimed at, there is a good chance you are no longer in that spot. The Gazelle is only just under 10 metres long at its widest aspect side on, most other aspects would only be four to five metres with perhaps a tree or building in the way as well.

The next weapon didn't need aiming to perfection; it found you!

Introduced into US Army service in 1981, The General Dynamics FIM-92 Stinger was a Man Portable Air Defence System capable of seeking an aircraft's heat source up to 12,000ft. The Stinger ended the war for the Soviets in Afghanistan with 269 helicopters reportedly shot-down.

We didn't know at the time if PIRA had one or more of these formidable weapons, but it was greatly feared that they had, and I had no intention of finding out personally!

It was also reassuring to know that Lynx and Puma helicopters had been fitted with the AN/ALQ-144 IRCM (Infrared Counter Measures) pod but that our Gazelles were 'awaiting trials' at Boscombe Down due to their 'low' heat signature.

I bumped into Izzie later in the officer's mess and we exchanged pleasantries as normal people do even in extraordinary circumstances. On her way to the bar, we chatted about our different days at work, and I told her about the briefing and how it had impacted me personally.

*Love Shack* by the B-52s was drifting out from somewhere, I still cannot hear that song without being reminded of Ireland.

Her eyes narrowed and then softened 'Scary stuff. You cannot take it personally. It is what we signed up for I guess.' She was interrupted as she always was when she wanted to say something meaningful, but I knew what she meant. Why were any of us here? Did anything we did have any true definition in the history of decades of Irish conflict. I loved flying but was I prepared to give my life for it?

The unspoken code of conduct bottled it all up inside.

Izzie excused herself from the bar and drifted away and I finished my beer. I started to get angry with myself for feeling anything other than the desire to please and do my duty and live up to the life I had wanted as an Army pilot.

I was determined to stay focussed, but it became harder and harder for us all.

# 7

# Night Stalkers

The short flight to Lisanelly Barracks in the centre of Omagh was uneventful. It was dusk and Sergeant Dan Weston and I were rostered together to crew Gazelle Six equipped with the FINCH surveillance camera. Dan approached from the south in a descending right turn picking up the landing site, the main barracks square. Omagh is the county town of Tyrone situated where the rivers Drumragh and Camowen meet to form the Strule.

Omagh was home to the 6th Battalion of the Ulster Defence Regiment (UDR), and we were there to support them this evening. High-level cloud and light north-westerly winds were forecast meaning good flying conditions.

We landed behind a Lynx on the square with the main row of vehicle hangars to our right, home to all of the many Land Rovers and some maintenance trucks. Dan completed the shutdown while I wrote 0.5 on my kneepad, 30 minutes flying time from Aldergrove.

Grabbing our helmets and flying gear we walked towards the battalion air tasking cell at the far end of the square. We both wore our cold weather flying jackets on top of our flying suits; underneath were the crew vests that contained all the ammunition and other survival bits and pieces such as field dressings. There was activity at the far end where two pairs of Land Rovers were being loaded with equipment and soldiers were milling about chatting and joking.

I had immense respect for the men and women of the UDR. Predominantly a part-time force, these people would finish their daytime jobs, don uniform and turn out to do an evening shift as a UDR soldier. The UDR were the mainstay of framework operations in the province, denying PIRA freedom of movement on the streets and roads and guarding key installations. In terms of experience, their intimate knowledge of their own country, of those who engaged in terrorism, of where previous attacks had taken place and previous finds had been made. They were better suited to many tasks than the Regular units sent to Northern Ireland on four-month, later to become six-month tours.

However, this admirable contribution came at a brutal cost. One hundred and ninety-seven members of the UDR lost their lives, with hundreds more injured. The intimidation they underwent was relentless and I was proud to help them tonight in their task. The four vehicles lined up at the top end of the square had just driven in from the nearby St Lucia barracks in the town.

The Ops Sergeant on duty from the Worcestershire and Sherwood Foresters, who were the resident battalion at Lisanelly, looked up from the TV in the corner and pointed in the direction of the troops outside, 'Your mission should you choose to accept is to provide top cover for those guys. Whisky One Alpha is the multiple leader with two Land Rovers and Whisky One Bravo is the other one. Your callsign is Nighthawk One on Channel 12.[1] Will you be requiring fuel Sir so I can warn off the duty refueller? The Lieutenant will be here shortly to brief you.'

As he spoke, the UDR patrol commander walked into the office and introduced himself. In his 40s, he would be a little old to hold that rank in the Regular Army, but good grief, they even had 50-year-old Privates!

> 'So, I've got two callsigns, there will be two VCPs [Vehicle Check Points] set up, one on the B22 towards Fintona at this grid reference here and one on the B83 on the Seskinore Road. Standard VCP drill. I've got 15 men and one Greenfinch [a member of the Women's UDR]. We will give it about an hour there and then move further down towards Clogher and give it another hour there. We will probably use the main A5 to get back in.'

I asked him if there was any particular reason for these locations and he replied that there was some intelligence about weapons hidden near Clogher, only three miles from the border and these roads might be used to bring a weapon into Omagh itself. I told him we would launch and clear the two roads ahead of his convoy of four vehicles which would then split just south of Omagh into two patrols of two vehicles each. I reminded him that we would show no lights and asked if there were any other friendly teams out on the ground in the area. There weren't as far he knew and nowhere surrounding was 'out of bounds' at the moment meaning no Special Forces ops were in place.

Having agreed a departure time with the UDR officer, I marked up my map while Sergeant Weston went outside to start up.

'Have a good one' grinned the desk sergeant, 'I have taken the liberty of ordering you both a couple of meals for when you get back' and he went back to watching Eastenders. I had forgotten that we both hadn't had a chance to eat before leaving Aldergrove. 'By the way, the Greenfinch is Lieutenant Robinsons wife!'

The troops were lined up at the weapons bay as I walked out to the Gazelle and on the word of command loaded their SA80 rifles.

---

1   'Nighthawk Boom': The sound that the nighthawk bird makes when stalking its prey.

RE Officers Full Dress Tunic 1902-1939. (Museum of Army Flying, with permission)

Bristol Boxkite Replica 'No 12', The Shuttleworth Collection (CC BY-SA 2.0, ©Eric Jones)

Middle Wallop airfield. (Author's photo)

Gazelle XZ305 on Spot One at Bessbrook HLS. (Author's photo)

RAF Wessex landing at Bessbrook HLS. (Author's photo)

Gazelle AH 1. (Author's photo)

Gazelle, view from the cockpit. (Author's photo)

Sturgan Mountain and Sugarloaf with Slieve Gullion behind. (Author's photo)

Gazelle over Belfast. (Public Domain)

Lynx AH 7 cockpit. (Author's photo)

Author's flying chart of Northern Ireland. (Author's photo)

VII

Gazelle in hover. Note twin VHF-FM homing aerials. (Author's photo)

Author 1990. (Author's photo)

A photo taken in 2018 of a 665 Squadron Gazelle equipped with a thermal imaging camera on the starboard boom. (Tim Felce)

Bessbrook HLS today. (Author's photo)

New control tower at Enniskillen Airport. (Author's photo)

Croslieve Mountain. (Author's photo)

Sturgan Mountain and Sugarloaf from Cam Lough. (Author's photo)

MH-6 'Little Bird' with author at the controls. (Author's photo)

Sergeant Weston had completed the pre-flight and we started up. I loaded the map coordinates he had given me into the LWNA and loaded the FINCH monitor with a blank cassette tape. Switching the power to ON, it whirred into life, and I tested the gimballing turret using the hand controller. Satisfied that it was working correctly, I called on the radio:

'Whisky One Alpha and Whisky One Bravo, this is Nighthawk One radio check over'

Both callsigns checked in and I called their Ops Room:

'Whisky Zero this is Nighthawk One lifting in two minutes over.'

'Whisky Zero Roger out.'

I then switched to Flight Safety Common on the UHF radio to warn any other helicopters in the vicinity:

'Yankee Zero One One, Gazelle lifting in the overhead, Yankee Zero One One.'

'Clear left.'

'Clear right.'

Weston pulled up on the collective and I followed him through on the controls as he lifted into the hover and then climbed out over the brightly lit town. We orbited a couple of times at 1,000ft while I got my bearings and found the road leading south out of Omagh.

'Ok I have control, you get onto NVG and when you are ready let me know.'

Once he was set, I handed control back and started to focus on the monitor in front. I positioned the camera forward and about 45 degrees angled down to cover the ground ahead.

Thermal imagers are camera systems which collect radiation from that part of the spectrum where objects emit heat. They operate in the infrared part of the spectrum, at longer wavelengths than visible light. The images they produce use differences in the thermal radiation emitted by the objects in the scene ahead. However, the systems rely on temperature differences: no difference, no image. Outdoor conditions are rarely ideal but tonight was about as good as it gets.

None of us were experienced camera operators if I am honest. We were soldier pilots with limited training on the system, but everyone thought we were expert at operating.

In order to present heat in a format useful to the human eye, thermal imagers convert the temperature of objects into shades of grey which are darker or lighter than the background. These shades of grey are displayed as an image. The sensitivity of the camera is typically described by the minimum resolvable temperature difference that can be detected. For these reasons, thermal cameras have become a useful tool for surveillance because generally, at night, background objects tend to be cooler than a person. Under ideal conditions, people are clearly emphasised at night because they appear brighter than the background and stand out, even in zero light.

Once away from the lights of the town we climbed to 1,500ft and I scanned the camera along the road, located the junction where the two patrols would divide and continued forward. The proposed VCPs were both only about two miles outside Omagh on two small country lanes. I flew the camera slowly down both lanes looking at the layout of the surrounding fields and farms.

An occasional car travelled down the road, its bonnet glowing white with the heat from the engine, cows in the fields were scattered in groups as white objects, farmhouse roofs stood out against the grey background. My pilot colleague was seeing all this too through his goggles but in green!

I called up Whisky One Alpha and told him he was clear to depart.

The convoy of four vehicles made their way out of the front gate, there was a slight delay as they were all checked out and then turned south towards the main A5 road to Ballygawley The traffic was light and after about 10 minutes the convoy reached Doogary where the junction with the B road turned south. Following this minor road for about half a mile, the road forked and the lead vehicle turned right towards Fintona, while Whiskey One Bravo continued.

We continued circling overhead at 1,500ft tracking their movements. I had switched the red, green and white external navigation lights off as well as the anti-collision lights on the tail of the cab. We were now invisible from the ground and to other aircraft, so I put out regular calls on the UHF of our position. Other aircraft are usually easily spotted by their flashing strobe anti-collision light rather than the fixed fainter navigation lights on both sides of the fuselage.

The two mobile patrols had now reached their pre-determined sites and they both started setting up their VCPs which had to be done in a set way to comply with Road Traffic Regulations and the UDR were the Army's experts.

Blocking off one side of the road with one vehicle, the other vehicle would be positioned metres down the road blocking the other side to create a secure box in which the car checks could be done. Occupants could be questioned, and cars searched while sentries took up firing positions up and down the road and to each side. VCPs were never set up next to houses or farm buildings for obvious reasons.

Up above we were an extra pair of eyes and provided reassurance to the soldiers below that there were a couple of people on their side looking out for them. In reality we could only observe so much, and we were a deterrent more than anything. What PIRA gunman would choose to attack this patrol knowing we could track his every move on camera?

I zoomed the camera in on Whiskey One Bravo and saw they were nicely in position on a section of road just before it entered a small forest. I could clearly see each member of the patrol by their white heat signature and counted eight men in total. Now it was just a matter of sit and wait.

I checked on the other patrol with the camera and then we moved down towards Fintona to check for any vehicles approaching. Dan was using the NVG to pick up the road layout which otherwise would have been completely invisible in the darkness. Ahead were the yellow sodium lights of Fintona and further west I could pick out Enniskillen and the glistening silvery shape of Lower Lough Erne, a beautiful part of the county of Fermanagh.

Towards the south-east about 4 miles (6 km) away, about halfway between Fintona and the village of Fivemiletown, the land rises to the summit of Murley Mountain, better known locally as 'Fivemiletown Mountain', which has a peak of 312 metres (1,024ft) above sea level.

I glanced over to Dan and commented that Fintona had a small RUC station but nothing else. Besides flying the helicopter, maintaining height and speed Dan would have been scanning the terrain below for likely landing sites if we had to put down in an emergency.

Our fast and nimble Gazelle had one disadvantage compared to all the other types of military helicopter flying in the province. It only had one engine.

Yes, the single Turbomeca Astazou 3NA turboshaft engine was extremely reliable but in practice could quit at any moment. Unlike twin-engine helicopters such as the Lynx and Wessex which could continue to fly on the remaining engine while a restart could be attempted, we had to continuously be on the alert of losing the engine for whatever reason. We were taught to recognise an engine failure in the cruise by a slight yaw and roll to the right along with zero torque on the torquemeter and of course the noise rolling back from its constant whine behind your head. Autorotation or 'windmilling' downwards is made possible because of the freewheel unit which allows the rotor system to disengage itself from the engine drive system when the engine speed through the reduction gear is less than the rotor rpm. This action is automatic and built into the transmission, but the blades are still angled to the airflow and will very rapidly slow down with nothing driving them unless this pitch angle is reduced immediately by lowering the collective lever fully by the pilot.

Hammered into us during training, and with multiple practice autorotations logged, it was almost second nature to carry out this action of entering autorotation with one big difference: we almost always knew it was coming due to the constraints of safe flying training regulations, but if it happened for real, with all the other myriad of distractions and fatigue in flying a helicopter any delay might prove fatal. It is interesting to note that more Gazelles were written off in practice engine-off exercises than were ever lost in genuine failure of the Astazou engine!

Obviously you wanted to give yourself as much time as possible to select a suitable field, so a certain airspeed gave you the maximum time but if you needed to clear obstacles such as built-up areas or high ground, a higher speed would increase the distance you could travel at the expense of a higher rate of descent. The airflow would now be coming up through the spinning rotors rather than being forced downwards but you could still control the revolutions by raising the collective slightly to prevent overspeed and maintain the design limitations.

Flying around built-up areas, sports fields with floodlights were great potential landing sights, but in rural areas any flattish ground would have to do.

I radioed through to Whisky One Bravo, the second patrol, 'vehicle heading north towards your position.' Just giving them a few minutes notice of a visitor was a significant help in this situation as they hardly had any vehicles through their checkpoint so far.

'He's stopping short.' Dan said.

The vehicle which I could see was an estate car and had clearly stopped just before emerging from the line of trees at the edge of the forest.

'Try and get me in a position where I can read the reg.' I would have to have the camera facing straight down the road on full magnification if I was going to have any chance of success. The occupants of the vehicle clearly wanted to avoid going through the VCP and had now started reversing back along the road. I could no longer see the vehicle clearly due to the trees. Another vehicle was now entering the forest from the other direction having passed through the checkpoint. Avoiding a checkpoint wasn't a crime but was certainly suspicious to say the least.

'Go to the junction where the forest road ends,' I ordered Dan and then quickly radioed the patrol commander what was happening. The UDR was in no position to commence high speed chases through country lanes at night and in any case, it could be a normal citizen spooked at the prospect of being questioned or searched rather than a hardened terrorist. I thought if I could at least get the registration number of the vehicle, I could radio it in to Whisky One Alpha, the lead callsign and the Lieutenant could run it through a 'Vengeful' DVLA check. However, that would take time.

We were starting to stray from my job which was to provide top cover to my UDR mobile patrol, and I was conscious of the conflict of this distraction with the main task. However, if some information could be gained by following the vehicle, then it would be a bonus to the intelligence gathering community.

At the other end of the forest, we waited hovering now still at 1,500ft for the vehicle to reappear on my screen monitor, but nothing appeared. He should have been through by now, and now the other vehicle appeared and turned towards Fintona. Had he seen the estate car in the forest? There was no way of knowing.

I was mystified. It had just disappeared without trace, not even a heat signature from the engine. There could only be one answer, they must have entered a garage or barn to hide and if so, why? What were they trying to hide?

I radioed the Lieutenant 'Whisky One Alpha this is is Nighthawk One, suspect vehicle lost, do your guys know of any buildings in the forest south of Whisky One Bravos position. Over.'

A few minutes later, the Lieutenant called back to say someone in the patrol knew of a derelict timber yard in that area. Timber drying sheds are large enough to park underneath, perhaps they were hiding under cover to avoid being identified.

I was not in command of this operation, only my helicopter, but I reasoned that if the patrol commander would move his mobile to the other end of the forest where it met the junction to the south of where Whiskey One Bravo was, the vehicle would not be able to leave the area without going through the security check. I quickly suggested my plan to the UDR commander. The B83 road out of the forest ended just outside the village of Seskinore and soon enough Whiskey One Alpha were packing up and preparing to move. I estimated a journey time of no more than five minutes if he took a ridiculously small lane running southeast direct to the village, longer if he chose to stay on the B road.

Would he manage to pack up move location and set up again before the suspicious estate car moved off again? It was a game of cat and mouse now and a race against time.

'Boss, we've been airborne nearly an hour,' Sergeant Dan reminded me. I glanced at the fuel gauge, still approximately another 45 minutes maximum before refuelling. 'We cannot stay here forever.'

I agreed, this was normally approaching the upper limit we would allocate to one task and operating the camera continuously was fatiguing. There was no way of swapping duties as the FINCH equipment was all on the Aircraft Commander's side and partially obscured the view through the Perspex bubble.

We couldn't be in two places at once, so I prioritised the mission in favour of monitoring the patrol commander's move to his new location. At least that way if the shit hit the fan, I still had eyes on him rather than on an unverified but potentially hostile entity.

The patrol commander wisely chose the longer, less risky route to Seskinore but it was taking a good deal longer than five minutes. It was pitch dark, they were probably fumbling with maps, and I could see they were following a slow-moving tractor with his lights blazing and towing a small trailer. My heart sank, what if I had led them into a trap?

'Whisky One Alpha, move back from the vehicle in front, I repeat move back from the vehicle in front!'

This was too coincidental to be a planned attack, but you could never be sure. The tractor reached the Seskinore junction and turned right towards Fintona. About 100 metres behind, the mobile now sped up and turned left towards the village. This was going to work!

The distance to Seskinore was now only two miles, I checked ahead and radioed an all clear. Dan was doing an expert job of keeping the cab positioned and we flew ahead to recce the forest again for any further movement. The forest was a grey collection of conifers and woodland with some minor tracks running off at angles to the main road. I scanned these carefully for white objects: anything white would indicate a person or animal in amongst the undergrowth.

Suddenly, the estate car appeared heading south at full speed towards Seskinore, no headlights and kicking up a trail of dust behind the vehicle.

'Whisky One Alpha secure' followed by the map coordinates.

That's what I wanted to hear.

'Whisky One Bravo this is Nighthawk One, Whisky One Alpha secure in new location. Target now moving south towards Seskinore high speed. Do you copy?'

I relayed the situation to the other VCP still in their position in case they couldn't receive their patrol commander's message.

A distinct Northern Irish accent replied 'Roger aye.' I followed the estate car as it slowed towards the new VCP set up just off the village high street where the streetlights began. As if nothing had happened it pulled into the VCP and stopped in front of two soldiers kneeling aiming their weapons at the car. A third approached and covered the rear.

I loitered scanning the area around for a possible ambush. All quiet. The patrol commander radioed in that he was happy to release us and I could see the estate car had its tailgate open and was being searched. The patrol commander was going to stay at this location as long as it took to complete the Vengeful check and then return to Omagh using the main A5 road from Ballygawley.

We headed back towards Omagh.

'Mind if I take it?' I said following through on the controls. It was a relief to fly the helicopter after time peering at the screen. There was nothing for Dan to do so I asked him to do the Ops Normal and task complete call back to Aldergrove while I pondered the situation. During the time the vehicle had 'disappeared' had they had a chance to hide a weapon or bomb making equipment in that location or were they just spooked?

Perhaps they were our guys who didn't want their cover blown?

We were never given any information on covert operations and there was a lot of that going on at any one time especially in this East Tyrone area of the province as well as Belfast.

I started a descending left turn into the barracks picking out the red light on the comms mast and the sodium lights lining the vehicle sheds. Completing the night landing checks, I felt for the landing light switch on the collective and switched the external lights back on. Bit steep I thought, so I eased right slightly to widen my left turn and swung inside the high grey security fence to flare over the square. Ahead I could see the Lynx had departed so I hover taxied to the top end to leave space on the other landing spots. Funny, I thought, I never heard their departing call, I must have been too engrossed at the time.

I shut down and the noise and vibration died away. It was all quiet inside the base. I ejected the VCR tape from the monitor unit, switched off the camera and walked to the Ops Room while Dan completed the post-flight inspection and waited for the refueller to arrive.

I went inside where my friendly Ops sergeant was still watching TV. 'Ok Sir? Refueller is on his way. I've got nothing else for you tonight. The meals are in the fridge for you both in the crew room…that is if the Lynx crew haven't scoffed them, there is a microwave in there.'

I wanted to know if there was any update with the UDR patrol.

'They are on their way back in, they said to thank you guys for an excellent job tonight.'

I handed him the VHS videotape and he scribbled an entry into the log. 'There, a bit of light entertainment for you' I mused. 'The Int cell will have a look at that tomorrow.' He grinned.

'And the vehicle, any news on the estate car we stopped?'

'Oh yes, both local men with known PIRA connections, nothing found though. Had to let them through.'

Shaking my head, I went into the crew rest area next door and went straight to the small fridge in the corner. It was empty.

# 8

# Deadly Down

County Down is where, in the words of the song by Percy French, 'The mountains of Mourne sweep down to the sea.' As one of the two counties in Northern Ireland to have a Protestant majority, it was an area considered relatively safe to the Security Forces. The well-heeled contingent had large houses in the popular towns of Bangor, Newtownards, and Downpatrick. It takes its name from *dún*, the Irish word for dun or fort, which is a common root in Gaelic place names (such as Dundee, Dunfermline and Dumbarton in Scotland and Donegal and Dundalk in Ireland)

The main fort in the area, as far as we were concerned, was at Ballykinler in the south of the county about eight miles south-west of Downpatrick. It was a large training camp known as Abercorn Barracks and home to the Northern Ireland Reinforcement Training Team which ran compulsory courses for all new arrivals posted into NI. Its main asset was extensive firing ranges which stretched out toward the coastal fringes of Dundrum Bay with the spectacular backdrop of the Mourne Mountains. It was one of my favourite locations in the province.

Not so for the Republican movement. In the aftermath of Bloody Sunday on 21 November 1921, the British authorities arrested hundreds of Republicans and opened several internment camps throughout Ireland, and Ballykinler was the first one to be used. Over the following year 2,000 men were interned there and the camp had a reputation for brutality: three prisoners were shot dead, while five died from maltreatment.

Besides the training team, there was another Regular resident battalion based there, the 1st Battalion, the Black Watch as well as 3rd Battalion UDR and some other supporting units.

One morning I was on duty at Bessbrook with Gazelle Four when a call came into Buzzard Ops about a serious incident in 39 Infantry Brigade's TAOR (Tactical Area of Responsibility). All non-operational vehicle movement in the area was to stop immediately. Up until then, it had been a quiet couple of hours since we had flown from Aldergrove earlier that morning.

'Gazelle, can you get airborne and go straight to Lisburn and shutdown.'

'You will be briefed when you get there.'

Something bad had happened, perhaps a kidnapping or a shooting at a checkpoint, I thought as I walked out of the portacabin towards the Gazelle sitting on its customary spot a few metres away in the pouring rain. My colleague was a warrant officer pilot also an Aircraft Commander and I was flying right seat today.

Bessbrook to Lisburn was about 20 miles which meant no more than 12–15 minutes flying time. WO Kenny told me that another Gazelle was enroute to Lisburn from our squadron base at Aldergrove and we were to land next to it on the sports field which doubled up as the helicopter landing site. Someone at the headquarters had decided that there should be a recce team available there for whatever had happened.

Starting up the engine for the second time today, I made sure the ENG Ground Idle light on the panel was extinguished, and then checked the rpm and T4 had stabilised before 'uncaging', that is to say unlocking the standby artificial horizon and switching on the heater in the probe that registered our speed to prevent it icing up.

WO Kenny switched on both wipers to clear the windscreen and I went ahead with the rotor engagement. One thing we never compromised on or rushed was this strict sequence of checks written on our Flight Cards, usually held in a plastic sleeve in the flying suit knee pad.

Rotors turning now, wipers running, the noise was incredible as usual. I think one of my helmet seals needed replacing. I made a mental note to take it in for servicing if I would ever get a chance. Kenny checked his map while I unlocked the main gyro instruments, checked everything was within limits, put the NAV lights to STEADY, everything with the left hand. You never took your hand off the cyclic with the rotors turning.

With the rain belting down, we lifted into the hover, I did a quick pedal turn to the right to clear behind and above and pulled up on the collective. Rising higher, I pushed in the righter pedal to keep straight, up, up clearing the fence now and once I could see the houses and fields outside the base eased the cyclic a fraction of an inch to get her moving forward. Quick check of the torquemeter, ease forward more and correct the little sink towards the ground with collective.

As the forward speed registered a few knots on the airspeed indicator, the rotor blades advancing on the left side of the aircraft got more airflow and more lift force than the retreating blades on the right. This would logically roll the helicopter right and because everything on the rotor disc happens a whole quarter turn of the blades later, the effect was to tilt the spinning disc backwards not forwards. Uncorrected the helicopters nose would pitch up and just slow back to a hover again, so anticipating I progressively eased further forward on the cyclic to keep accelerating.

As the helicopter gathers speed the power required to maintain level flight reduces and can be felt as a little shudder through the airframe as the machine accelerates even more without further movement of any of the controls. Up and away! Crossing the railway line at 100ft on the radio altimeter, I turned north to follow the Newry River.

Kenny gave me a running commentary from the left seat. The ground is rushing past in a green blur at 90 knots airspeed. Equivalent to 100 miles per hour, your eyes are outside the cockpit looking ahead horizontally as far as possible to follow features to navigate by. This nap of the earth technique is unique to military flying. Civilian helicopters as well as fixed wing aircraft must by law fly at least 500ft above all obstacles or risk prosecution.

A small town came up very quickly to the left of the river and Kenny pointed right towards a large town in the distance. The rain had cleared now, and I eased up on the collective as the ground was rising away from the river valley.

A large road was coming in from the right-hand side, the main dual carriageway A1 from Newry was full of vehicle traffic now throwing up a lot of spray. We were double their speed at least but it didn't feel that way.

'Wires ahead,' called Kenny.

Huge 200ft pylons marched across the countryside ahead converging with the road.

I jinked left and climbed the Gazelle aiming for the nearest one at about a 45-degree angle, that way if we had a problem such as a bird strike, I could turn away from them increasing the rate of turn to avoid the wires running between them. We always crossed wires at the mast or pole, which was the drill. Having safely negotiated the National Grid, we crossed the A1 and flew south of the Long Kesh prison camp, the ground climbing all the time past the hilltop village of Hillsborough, slowing back to 60 to 70 knots as the main mass of housing marking Lisburn approached to the north.

Thiepval Barracks was also the HQ of the British Army in Northern Ireland. Full of high-ranking officers, it was typical rear echelon with sports fields, schools, swimming pool and plenty of housing for the families stationed here. I know of many Army members who never even left the base once during a tour. The security here was massive with permanent VCPs on every possible approach to the barracks.

'Victor Zero One Zero, Gazelle landing one minute from the south.'

I approached steeply to a high hover over the sports field and landed on the side nearest a road with some benches overlooking the grass.

Shutting down we stepped out, sat on one of the benches and waited.

The Brigade Commander and his Chief of Staff, a lieutenant colonel in the Royal Green Jackets arrived in their staff car on the road behind us. Striding over to us, we of course stood up and saluted. By now we had replaced our flying helmets with the headdress of the Army Air Corps, the light blue beret. I was proud to have the yellow grenade flash of the Corps of Royal Engineers sown onto mine signifying I was from another part of the Army.

Looking pale, the Chief of Staff briefed us that there had been a culvert bomb incident near Downpatrick involving the UDR and there had been 'multiple casualties.'

The Brigade Commander wanted to have a quick airborne recce of the scene before visiting the CO of the UDR battalion at Ballykinler. We would then wait there and bring them back. He explained breathlessly that the area was presently out of bounds and was being cleared by Royal Engineer search teams for possible secondary devices designed to kill further patrols.

Strapping into the Gazelle, I waited for Mr Kenny to finish assisting our high-ranking passengers into the rear seats. They would have flown many times so were familiar with all the headsets and door jettisoning procedure. The Brigadier General sat behind me, and they had a mobile telephone in what seemed like a small suitcase in between them. We took off and climbed as high as possible away from the security of the most heavily guarded barracks in the province.

Downpatrick lies at the southern end of a large, beautiful lake called Strangford Lough, and has a racecourse so it would be easy to find. Kenny called Belfast Approach radar because the direct route took us through the airspace controlled by Belfast City Airport, we were cleared up to 2,500ft and I increased power on the collective to the highest setting giving us about 120 knots or 2 miles a minute.

I slowed and descended to a safe altitude of 1,500ft and located the Ballydugan road running out of Downpatrick. On a straight single-carriage road just past the racecourse, there was a scene of utter carnage. A vehicle utterly unrecognisable as a Land Rover had been blown 30 metres over a hedge into a field and was now just blackened twisted metal. Another Land Rover was stopped in the road of about 20 metres past a huge crater in the road. We orbited a while for our top brass passenger to digest the scene below.

There were a couple of RUC vehicles much further back diverting traffic and there was a recovery vehicle of some sort as well being escorted towards this Land Rover. I find it hard to describe the feeling of anger and shock of witnessing the aftermath of an attack like this on our guys.

I remember thinking that a huge amount of explosive must have been used and the timing perfect to carry out this atrocity. We orbited the site, and it was clear this was a culvert bomb. How is it possible to place such a massive amount of explosive under a road and not be noticed? Why when culverts are such an obvious place to hide explosives are they not checked on a regular basis? Why was this patrol going to Downpatrick anyway? What was the point of their task today? I was lucky not to be the Brigade Commander I thought because he would have to answer and justify all these answers up the chain to higher command.

When we landed at Ballykinler Camp we found out that it had indeed been a patrol from 3 UDR and four brave soldiers had died in the explosion. They were Private John Birch (28), Lance Corporal John Bradley (25), Lance Corporal Michael Adams (23) and Private Steven Smart (23). The other four members of the patrol in the front Land Rover had survived and were being treated in a hospital in Belfast along with two civilians who were caught up in the blast. Apparently, there had been warnings that PIRA were preparing to mount a major strike in the area and the Ballydugan road was imminently about to be placed out of bounds.

It was late in the day when we took our passengers back to Lisburn and Mr Kenny and I flew back in silence to Aldergrove. I couldn't see how we could have prevented this happening even if we had been tasked with providing top cover for the patrol. As far as I could make out, this was a repeat of so many other incidents in the past that that could possibly have been avoided at the hand of a deadly enemy.

May they rest in peace.

# 9

# All Along the Watchtowers

I had been pestering John, our squadron QHI, for what seemed like ages for a familiarisation flight in one of the Lynx helicopters operated by 665. It wasn't usually possible as the Lynx was always flown by two qualified Lynx pilots. I should explain, barring OCs and QHIs, the AAC didn't allow you on more than one type. You were trained on the Gazelle and either stayed on the machine operationally or you undertook a Lynx Conversion Course at Middle Wallop. When it came to the end of my pilot's course, we were given the chance to express a preference one way or another but like most things in the Army, the 'needs of the service' took priority. Aware that the majority of Lynx at that time were in Germany and that expressing a desire to fly one meant an almost certain posting there, as my wife's job and our house was in Hampshire I elected to remain on the trusty Gazelle.

Eventually John agreed. 'What are you doing this afternoon?' he said over breakfast one morning.

'Day off,' I replied.

'Right, I've got to do an air test at 2pm' he said without looking up, 'I will have to clear it with Sam but if you hang around the crew room and wait until the REME have finished, come out onto the pan, no weapons please, and you owe me a beer by the way.'

And that was it. He went back to his scrambled eggs and bacon and the Sun newspaper.

All I knew about operating the Lynx came from my mate Steve Harrison, a Lynx pilot from the Royal Green Jackets, over chats in the bar. We got on well together I suspect because we were both not badged Army Air Corps and we covertly liked to have a laugh at some of their idiosyncrasies. He used to talk about ECLs and Nh and Nf and governor runaways and made it sound very mysterious. I just had to have a go.

The Westland Lynx AH Mk1 was introduced into Army service in 1979 or thereabouts so it hadn't been around that long. There was a Royal Navy version painted grey, but curiously no civilian version. Powered by two Rolls Royce Gem turbines, it was altogether a more complex proposition than the Gazelle. The Army used it for carrying up to nine troops (alive or dead), and for firing anti-tank missiles from, that was basically it.

There were loads of differences. Apart from having two engines, the four-bladed semi-rigid rotor turned to the left, the other way to the Gazelle. It had a distinctive buzz-burring sound as opposed to the whistling whining Gazelle and it was fast! Extremely fast. In testing it had logged over 200 knots in level flight I believe.

The first thing I noticed after climbing aboard and strapping in was the size of the cockpit. A central console separated the two seats and there were a lot more switch panels in the roof. In front of me in the left co-pilots seat was an identical air instrument panel to the Commander's, whereas the Gazelle had a central binnacle with just the one set. There was a windscreen rather than a bubble canopy and it felt like I had just climbed into a Sherpa van. After plugging my helmet into the intercom, John gave me the usual brief on the door emergency jettison and the fire extinguishers and then fired up the second engine by pressing the start switch on a roof-mounted lever and advanced it forward. He was talking through the procedure of starting the No 1 engine in accessory drive, then the No 2 engine, then checking the Flight Control System thoroughly before rotor start and then selecting MAIN DRIVE.

After the rotor rpm had been adjusted to 107 percent and the torques on both engines matched, he had to check the anti-icing system was OK as this was far more of an all-weather machine than the Gazelle, but it wasn't required today. Making sure the collective was set at Minimum Pitch on Ground, John allowed me to release the rotor brake slowly and spun up the rotors. The whole procedure seemed to take longer than what I was used to, but the rotors engagement was faster.

Aldergrove Tower cleared us to the south and John lifted into a hover and pedal-turned left and taxied out across the grass to the edge of the runway where he turned further into wind and took off towards Lough Neagh. The effect of the higher seating position and the recommended 10-foot hover height was alarming to say the least to this humble Gazelle pilot. Levelling at 2,000ft over the lake, John handed over control warning me that the cyclic was ultra-sensitive compared to the Gazelle. You can get high g-loadings building up if moving the cyclic stick too quickly in any direction. Another notable feature of the Lynx was its auto stabilisation system, you could fly 'hands-off'! That was unheard of in my machine where the cyclic stick had to be held at all times. With feet off the pedals, it would hold a heading and John also demonstrated a trick where the Lynx would maintain the height on the altimeter. A really useful function, especially for hovering at high altitude. After a few steep turns to pull a bit of g, time was up and John lowered the collective to the MPOG and autorotated down to 500ft to the south of the airfield on the lake shore. It was a great 20 minutes of flying and increased my respect tremendously for the pilots who were trained on it, but remarkably quite a few of them still said they preferred the hands-on flying qualities of the Lynx's smaller sister.

Steve caught me that night over dinner. 'How did it go? How did you feel flying a real helicopter mate? Pretty cool eh.'

'You will soon be going back to Sennelager Ranges, backwards and forwards…!' I joked and we left it there.

A week had passed since the land mine attack outside Downpatrick. The bomb had reputedly used 1,000 pounds of Semtex to create that size of crater and a general mood of pessimism pervaded the province. South Armagh had started like that with multiple road bombings that eventually led to the situation today of banning all vehicle movement south of an imaginary line from Newry to Newtonhamilton. There was a palpable fear that this line would eventually extend northwards across the whole of Northern Ireland and more regions would become no-go areas making logistical support a nightmare. The answer was increased awareness, surveillance, and route checking. Every commander was to survey his TAOR for the culverts and ditches under roads large enough to contain these amounts of explosive, clear them safe and then keep them safe by covert and overt surveillance. It was a massive task and would involve a large amount of top cover flying and troop carrying to support. To me it was logical: plot every large culvert from photoreconnaissance or detailed map inspections and then get on the ground and watch them day and night. But it was obvious as well that there were nowhere nearly enough resources to do that permanently, but at least send a message out there that something was being done.

The next day I was rostered Gazelle Four yet again, which meant tasking from 3 Brigade Headquarters in Drumadd Barracks, Armagh. This usually involved the South Armagh reinforcement battalion, currently one of the two Scots Guards battalions. In order to keep in touch with their units on the ground, senior police and army officers had to spend a great deal of time visiting them, asking questions and delving into problems. The junior leadership came at lance corporal level responsible for a four-man patrol or 'brick'.

However, to not have to start from scratch, each battalion sent an advance party to NI some weeks before the arrival of the main body. This always consisted of the CO, company commanders and other key personnel. Today, a major and his intelligence captain from another regiment in the UK who were due to take over from the guardsmen had requested a Gazelle to recce the South Armagh watchtowers, their locations, fields of view and manning issues. It was to be demanding mountain flying landing on hilltops and pinnacles to take place over one, possibly two days, depending on the weather.

The 12 Golf and Romeo surveillance towers were built in the 1980s by the Royal Engineers to serve a specific need. Their primary purpose was to enable the Army to conduct patrols with some degree of safety and specifically to defend the soldiers at Forkill and Crossmaglen who were very exposed near the border. Their antecedent were stone towers built 400 years earlier and still remain today such as Moyry Castle near Jonesborough. The castle was built to secure the pass by Lord Mountjoy, Queen Elizabeth's most effective and ruthless general, who was sent to Ulster to crush the power of Hugh O'Neill, Earl of Tyrone. In May and October 1600, Mountjoy's armies advanced north into the pass through bogs, streams, and dense woods. On both occasions they returned via Carlingford, the lesser of two evils.

Two huge military efforts, codenamed Operations Condor and Magistrate were required to move massive amounts of raw materials and equipment to construct them. In 1980 during my first tour in Northern Ireland, I had acted as a convoy commander in an armoured Land Rover in a similar large operation known as Operation Tonnage to deliver stores to reinforce and expand the two bases. I had no idea that 10 years later I would be back to continue the work but in a quite different vehicle. Starting as little more than huts perched on flimsy scaffolding, the towers developed into much more substantial brick and mortar installations housing sophisticated equipment such as cameras, telescopes, communications aerials, and ground movement radar. They were also patrol bases allowing troops to move out on the ground directly without giving away their position by helicopter insertion undertaken by Lynx or the noisy RAF Wessex. The downside, apart from the cost of construction and maintenance, was the hatred they generated from the local population who saw them as symbols of colonial oppression. The Golf towers, about the height of a four-storey building, overlooked the border in South Armagh. There were only about 20 official road crossings between North and South in the whole province, all had permanent VCPs. The minor roads had been cratered, spiked, or blocked since 1971 but the paramilitaries could still easily slip across hedges and fields back into the South. The line divided rivers, bridges and occasionally sliced through individual houses.

The most notorious crossing was the 'gap of the North' between Black Mountain and Feede Mountain which leads through the Ring of Gullion from Leinster to Ulster. It was a main route of invasion throughout Irish history and many English soldiers lost their lives 400 years earlier in skirmishes and ambushes here. More recently, two senior RUC officers, Chief Superintendent Harry Breen and Superintendent Bob Buchanan, returning from a meeting in Dundalk in the South were shot dead on the Edenappa Road which runs north of the crossing in an IRA ambush a year earlier in 1989.

Another deadly place was the three miles of the A1 road between Cloghoge and Killeen, known as 'bomb alley' because 20 people had been killed there in the last five years. The permanent checkpoint here was a war zone and was overlooked by Romeo One Four, a watchtower which had a covered walkway down to the vehicle search bay and sangar called Romeo One Five. It was this tower with its tiny helipad that our two passengers wanted to visit first, and then if we survived that encounter, on to see Romeo Two One on Jonesborough Mountain. I was still uneasy about a missile attack from an SA-7 or Stinger. We had still not yet been fitted with an infrared suppressor on the engine exhaust. They were slow to arrive and priority for IR defences were clearly being given to the larger types of helicopters at that time. I was concerned but kept my thoughts to myself.

Flying with me today was an RAF Flying Officer, Dominic Crisp, on attachment to the squadron. Dom or 'Crispie' was a lanky sort of guy and the reason he was here was that he was waiting to go on his Puma Conversion Course back in England and had volunteered to fly here with us rather than endure a six-month desk job which the RAF had lined up for him. He loved golf and was always to be seen swinging his clubs dangerously on the sports field next to the Officers Mess.

With a brisk westerly wind, we had departed Bessbrook and in no time we had covered the three miles south of Newry to the checkpoint. You could see it almost as soon as you left Bessbrook and all you had to do was follow the road south. The Cloghoge was more of a hill than a mountain and close to the road and railway line. We clattered in over the tops of queuing cars approaching into wind and keeping the little pad in sight, which was slightly lower than the hill summit on the west side. I manoeuvred against the downdrafts which were swirling over the summit, and I noticed the torquemeter red light blink once or twice as we touched down indicating maximum hover power. The pad was nothing more than a wooden platform about 20ft square and covered with chicken wire to provide some grip. It was constantly being re-laid as the skids tended to tear it up and it became dangerously loose.

Shutting down, Dom checked the passengers out safely and agreed no more than a 10-minute stay. I sat there in the gently rocking Gazelle being buffeted by the gusts and thought back to my Lynx ride. This landing site was unique in that it was Gazelle-only due to its small dimensions. This cab was definitely more Jaguar E-type than Sherpa van!

Our passengers, a major and captain whose names I can no longer remember, came jogging down the trackway steps from the observation sangar accompanied by a fully suited and booted soldier guard with helmet and SA80. They strapped in the back and the soldier crouched in front of our Gazelle. He was far too close and in risk of being struck by the main rotor when we started up.

'Dumbshit!' exclaimed Dom waving him away. He's losing his head I thought, he's been cooped up here too long. Fifty-three lives were lost in Ireland by 'violent or unnatural causes' including suicides. It was a tragedy in itself. I started rotors and handed control to Dom, who really was too tall for this little helicopter, stretching his legs onto the pedals and lifted into the five-foot hover for a power check. We were on 90 percent torque which meant only just enough power margin for a tower transition so Dom pedal-turned left (a right turn would have incurred more power demand) and moved sideways off the pad into a little drop-off in the spur that the pad was on. We just hover taxied our way down the hillside keeping about 20ft above the ground until there was an unobstructed view ahead and then I felt the collective lever rise up, the nose dip and away we went accelerating and climbing to the south. It was unconventional to say the least but worked!

Skimming across the fields towards Jonesborough, a flat-topped piece of high ground dominated the view through the Perspex canopy. I pointed out the 800ft hill to the major sat in the back and reminded him that Romeo Two One was only about half a mile from the border at its closest point. It was more of a small army base than a watchtower. At its northern end was an isolated single storey sangar with what appeared to be a telescope on the roof looking north-east towards Camlough and Newry and then a few hundred metres at the southern end was a larger structure, a square box on top of scaffolding with olive green corrugated sheet cladding at least three storeys high. High-powered listening devices were mounted on tripods next to the box. There were numerous portacabins and masts dotted around a cylindrical water tower. The ground here was all brown bracken with patches of heather and bog contrasting with the green fields around. A short distance from the box sangar was a large communications mast bristling with aerials of all shapes and sizes. It looked like Moonbase Alpha from a science fiction novel and surrounding the entire site was a fence of double-stacked razor wire.

We put down on the obvious landing pad in the middle of the complex and since this was going to take longer than 10 minutes, agreed to do half an hour top cover over the site with the thermal image camera to see if we could spot anything the guys in the complex couldn't. Although a hilltop site like this has obvious advantages, there was plenty of dead ground (an area which cannot be seen) surrounding the hill and our time could be usefully employed in this task.

It was my turn to fly again as Dom would have to operate the camera from the left seat. Hands-on flying time was logged as '1st Pilot,' and all other time logged '2nd Pilot' apart from flying with an instructor which was always logged as 'Dual'. By this time in my humble career, I had only logged about 500 hours total, and about 100 hours of that time was 2nd Pilot, but I was gaining experience and confidence in a way that routine flying in England would never achieve so quickly.

On 17 February 1978, 12 years earlier, a Gazelle went down near this very location after being fired at by a Provisional IRA unit from the South Armagh Brigade. The IRA unit was involved in a gun battle with a Royal Green Jackets' observation post deployed in the area, and the helicopter was sent in to support the ground troops. The helicopter crashed after the pilot lost control of the aircraft while evading ground fire. The incident resulted in the death of Lieutenant Colonel Ian Douglas Corden-Lloyd, their CO. At the time he was the most senior British officer to be killed on active duty in Northern Ireland.

While we were in the hover overhead at 2,000ft, we heard a call from a Wessex of 72 Squadron inbound with an underslung load.

I heard him call 'Heavylift Five, inbound Romeo Two One from the north two minutes, Heavylift Five.'

No indication of altitude in the call, so Dom broke off his survey of the terrain below while we both scanned the skies around us for sight of the Wessex. I tried to face north but it was too difficult to hold the heading. The prevailing wind blowing up here at 2,000ft was about 30 knots from the west – nearly a gale – and every time the helicopter was not positioned facing the wind, I was blown sideways and it made it very difficult to hold position over the ground below, making Dom's job much harder than it already was.

Underslung loads were a common sight in Northern Ireland. Large nets containing boxes of ammunition, rations, vehicle spares, mail, and even laundry were constantly being moved down to Forkhill, Crossmaglen, and around the watchtowers. It was rare for a Gazelle or Lynx to be used in this role here because we had the Royal Air Force to do it for us – and they were exceptionally good at it too – however we had a few hours allocated on the pilot's course practising hooking up and flying circuits with the load attached.

You must be aware of the position of the load and its behaviour as well as its size in relation to the cable sling carrying it. Accurate flying was required to avoid the load and the aircraft swinging. If the helicopter starts to oscillate, it is usually counter-productive to try and oscillate in an opposing sense. Reducing speed by flaring gently or climbing usually cured a fore and aft swing while a sideways swing reduced if you turned steadily in the opposite direction to the swing of the load. If it all went horribly wrong, there was of course the guarded jettison switch on the collective lever to dump the load. For this reason, all towns and villages were avoided as much as possible!

'Visual,' called Dom and below us at about 500ft above the deck, the Wessex came into view. I loved the Wessex. As a cadet, it had been the first helicopter I had ever flown in while I was at a camp at RAF Gutersloh in Germany. It had a wheeled undercarriage so could do rolling take-offs and had a 'loadie' or Air Loadmaster in the back, usually a Flight Sergeant who knew his particular ship inside out. They were also operated by the Royal Navy as the HU5 version in large numbers, proving invaluable in the Falklands War.

'Have you ever flown the Wessex, Dom?' I asked my RAF colleague.

'Never have,' replied Dom 'I would have liked too though. I have never heard a bad word said about them.'

'Heavylift Two this is Gazelle Four, be advised we are in the hold 2,000ft above Romeo Two One,' Dom keyed the mike to let him know we were overhead.

'Och a teenie-weenie,' came the reply 'be careful up there, won't you!'

If they were listening in to our transmissions now PIRA knew there were two targets in one location, I thought. We didn't know if they monitored UHF communications at that stage, but it was always possible. There was little to report on the secure net direct to the watchtower OP commander, but he was grateful for the knowledge. We waited for the Wessex to unload his consignment and then swooped down in a gut-wrenching drop to the helipad to pick up our passengers who were waiting in the freezing wind by one of the sangars. They had no weapons or headgear and looked mighty vulnerable to sniper attack. Poor bastards, I thought, imagine getting shot before your tour had even started!

I took off to the north in the direction of Camlough following the route used by the Wessex who was heading tirelessly back to Dungannon for his second load of many that day. Our final destination was to recce Sturgan Mountain and Sugarloaf Hill, or as we knew them, Romeo One One and Romeo One Two, situated at the head of Camlough Lough. Along with its sister on Camlough Mountain on the other side of the lough, these 'backline posts' didn't overlook the border but instead the B134 Mountain Road leading into the heart of bandit country. Sugarloaf was a particularly aesthetic looking hill shaped like a pinnacle.

We flew around them at a low height to give the two guys an unobstructed view, but we wouldn't be landing there today. These two OPs were the responsibility of a different unit in the command, so we turned back towards Bessbrook Mill and watched the weather deteriorate. Lowering cloud and blustery winds heralded the arrival of a weather front over Armagh. We were needed at Dungannon now for another recce of some sort and we watched the Wessex take-off lumbering along with another underslung load towards Jonesborough. We were going to do a rotor only shutdown and then take-off immediately for our final task of the day. Settling on spot one, I pushed the collective down to its bottom stop, applied the locking friction with the twist grip and once my hand was free reached up and after cross-checking with Dom that I had the right lever, pulled back the yellow throttle to ground idle. Murphy's law said that if you could pull the wrong lever or flick the wrong switch, someday you would, so we always cross-checked vital controls especially when tired as we always were.

The engine wound down and we always stopped the rotors using the manual rotor brake controlled by a ROTOR red control handle next to the yellow throttle. Moving the handle out of the gated forward position and pulling downwards and backwards, and disc brakes were applied on the tail rotor shaft slowing the main rotor. The rotor was always stopped with one blade straight ahead ensuring the exhaust could not impact on either of the other two blades to the rear. Clever trick. When the rotor brake was on, a rod projecting from the side of the brake handle ensured you couldn't advance the throttle with the rotor brake still on.

At this stage, the engine is still running in ground idle, still noisy so Dom opens his door and gets out, opens the rear door, and helps the passengers disembark, locks the harnesses in the rear again, steps back in and closes his door. He then straps back in, plugs his helmet back into the intercom and we take stock. Dungannon is preprogrammed WP6 on the LWNA. I slew up to fix our position, release the rotor brake and advance the throttle to turn the noise on again. Into flight idle. Check left and right, nothing arriving or departing. Ground crew give a thumbs up, uncage the AI, frictions off, harnesses locked and then pull collective.

Enroute to Dungannon, we made our usual 'ops normal' call to Aldergrove who gave us a frequency to call the 8 UDR Battalion Ops Room for details. The police in Dungannon had received a telephone call to say there had been a small explosion in a van parked in an estate in the town. A call had been made earlier to the Parochial House (a Roman Catholic vicarage) by a member of the IRA stating there was a bomb in the van and 8 UDR were mounting a clearance operation. We were required to provide top cover to this clearance operation. There was no need to land at *Yankee Four Five Three* – the helicopter landing site at Killymeal House – which I had been into on a few occasions at night.

However, the weather was getting worse, and we could only manage about half an hour on the task before the poor visibility forced us to land at Dungannon where we took the opportunity to refuel and waited for an improvement in the weather. There were only four 'avgas outstations' in the province, all manned by Royal Air Force support units, at Ballykelly, St Angelo, Bessbrook and here at Dungannon. You were never more than 15 minutes flying time from a refuel which was a great relief to us pilots. Later we found out more details of the nearly deadly incident.

It transpired that the small explosion in the van was the detonator exploding prematurely while the device was being armed. At this stage, the bomber had fled the scene. The intended target had in fact been Killymeal House, the headquarters building belonging to 8 UDR and the van was an exact replica of one belonging to a construction firm that came daily into the compound and was intended to be driven into the base by an insider. The ATO (Ammunition Technical Officer) search team found 1,200lbs of homemade explosives, probably ammonium nitrate fertiliser and fuel oil, in the van; enough to destroy the base. It was a lucky escape for everyone.

# 10

# Cullyhanna

*I will go, I will go, when the fighting is over*
*To the land o' McLeod that I left to be a soldier.*
*I've a buckle on my belt, a sword in my scabbard,*
*A red coat on my back and a shilling in my pocket,*
*When we landed on the shore and saw the foreign heather,*
*We knew that some would fall and would stay there forever,*
*I will go, I will go.*

(Trad, translated from Gaelic)

The Dorsey Enclosure, or Na Dories – the gateways – is an extensive earthwork about 4km long which runs through the South Armagh area. The Dorsey Ramparts, or 'The Walls' as they are known locally, are said to have been a fortified frontier post to the kingdom whose capital was Emain Macha (Navan Fort), blocking an important historic route into South Armagh. It was built at a time when the power of the Ulster kingdom may have been at its strongest, around 100BC. Sometime later, Ulster was threatened from the south, and it is speculated that Dorsey may have been incorporated into a more extensive defensive system known in Monaghan and further west as the Black Pig's Dyke. With bogs, drumlins and small loughs to the west, and the Ring of Gullion to the east, the Dorsey was the only direct route from Dublin through to Ulster's capital.

Situated to the north-west, the Dorsey is the settlement of Cullyhanna. In early May, we started to receive a large amount of task requests to conduct observation and surveillance patrols centred on this one village. A major operation was being mounted by the Light Infantry in conjunction with the roulement companies in South Armagh. I went to the squadron Ops Room to find out more details. It was scant information at best. Two Armalites had been discovered hidden in a dry-stone wall at Sheetrim near Cullyhana in April. These two weapons had been involved in 17 killings going back to 1974. Weapons were being found all the time and were often left in place with tiny tracking devices placed so their movements could be followed leading to arrests.

Four arms shipments from Libya had brought a staggering amount of ordnance into the IRA's hands during the 1980s, culminating in the 1987 interception by French customs officers of the fifth shipment aboard the 237-ton freighter *Eksund* off Roscoff with its deadly cargo of 20 SA-7s, 10 DShKs, and 1,000 – yes, 1,000 –AK-47s!

I was tasked today with searching for two vehicles in the area, a red Vauxhall Cavalier and a blue Toyota van, and to report any sightings. They were suspected of being vehicles that the IRA used for transporting weapons locally. The Light Infantry had troops dug-in around Cullyhanna and Silverbridge and were hoping to intercept weapons being moved around and also to lure the IRA into attacking them. I flew down to Cullyhana with Sergeant Harris on 3 May and spent three fruitless hours circling and hovering overhead checking the lanes and byways around the village to the east of the Cullyhanna river south towards Drummill, and north as far as Newtonhamilton. It was a beautiful spring day, and the weather was starting to get better. What I was not aware of at the time, because it was kept secret, was that this was part of a bigger operation named Op Conservation involving the Scots Guards.

The thermal imaging camera, although it had good magnification, could not detect colour and I am sure there were people in the tasking cell who didn't appreciate this fact. The night 'cab' with a different crew went down there again that evening to conduct a further search, again without success. The next day I returned with Dom, and we concentrated our search further to the east along the Dorsey Road which ran straight as a die south-west to Silverbridge, another well-known Republican stronghold. It must be pointed out that this area of South Armagh was out of direct view of the Golf watchtowers and on higher ground. The nearest one being about three miles away.

For the troops on the ground in their foxholes, we were their only friends in that hostile killing ground. The operation was now to take on a new deadly turn for the worse.'

The main positions occupied by the Light Infantry were to be surrounded and watched by 16 concealed observation posts (OPs) belonging to the 2nd Battalion Scots Guards. The goal was to surprise and destroy any IRA unit attempting to penetrate the area. The troops were inserted by Lynx helicopter into an area of gorse in the early hours of 3 May. The IRA South Armagh Brigade watched these movements and was able to spot several of the hidden OPs. Eventually, they decided to attack one of the British positions at Slatequarry, near Cullyhanna, which was in the most vulnerable position. At 2 a.m. on 6 May, the exposed British position began to receive heavy fire from an IRA unit emplaced on the slope of a hill nearby. The OP was attacked with two 7.62 mm General Purpose Machine Guns and a Heckler & Koch G3 rifle; the latter used to cover the machine gun team's retreat towards Slatequarry Road, where a vehicle was waiting to pick them up. A bomb was planted between the OP and the road, to prevent any attempt to give chase. The IRA members fired their machine guns from rocky terrain next to an abandoned building. The shooting lasted some

90 seconds, and a total of 316 rounds were expended by the two sides. The section's leader, Lance Sergeant Graham Stewart was hit and died of wounds the following day.

On 6 May, the day of the attack, I was airborne again over the area providing top cover. The operation had been aborted and recovery of the troops on the ground had started. Lynx and Wessex crews flew in to pick-up points under considerable risk of a follow-up attack while I maintained a watch overhead. It was later acknowledged by PIRA that the presence of a helicopter forced them to cancel many planned attacks. They would have plenty of time to repeat the operation knowing we couldn't be airborne 24 hours a day.

Back at Aldergrove, a change to our flying program in South Armagh was announced by Sam. Wherever possible, Buzzard Ops down at Bessbrook would coordinate tasks so that we flew as pairs rather than individually so as to provide mutual support if one of us was brought down by a surface-to-air missile. Intelligence reports from informers and people in the know stated that a helicopter shootdown was the terrorists' highest priority. The Lynx had been equipped with the IRCM pod for two years now. Developed in the 1970s in response to US losses during the closing stages of the war in Vietnam to the Soviet SA-7 'Strela', this device redirects the infrared energy that a heat-seeking SAM homes in on, deflecting the missile off course. It consisted of a heated silicon carbide block that radiates a large amount of infrared energy. It is surrounded by a large cylindrical mechanical shutter that modulates the infrared output, producing a pulsing pattern. Early infrared guided missiles used a rotating reticule. When a target was not on the sensor's centreline, it would produce a pulse as the reticule swept over the target. When the target was on the sensor's centreline, the sensor would produce a constant signal as required by the early missiles to produce a 'lock on' that would allow a launch. The ALQ-144 produced a pattern of pulses that was approximately synchronised with the rotation rate of these reticules. Before launch this would prevent the missile actually locking onto the target, preventing the operator from firing the missile. After launch this would cause the missile to think that the target was off to one side and cause the missile to steer away from the aircraft carrying the IRCM.

That evening Izzie suggested going for swim at the garrison pool. I reluctantly accepted and was pleased to be in her company after a few stressful days flying. A strange thing happened while we were there swimming up and down the marked lanes. I recognised another colleague swimming in the other lane, who I knew as Ian. We had been forced to share a room for four months in the Falklands about five years ago. I began conversation but he cut off the chat abruptly voicing he was doing a tour with 'the Det' or 14 Intelligence Company and wasn't allowed contact with anyone for fear of compromise.

Izzie asked, 'Who was that strange guy in the pool with the long hair?'

'Ah just someone I used to know, who doesn't want to be known anymore,' I replied cagily.

'Oh, one of the sneaky beakies, they are a pain in the ass, almost as bad as pilots,' she laughed.

We walked back to the mess in the failing light.

'How much longer have you got?' She spoke.

'Another month, I want to stay … extend my tour but I don't think UK will allow it. Simply great here, finally doing a job for real, you know.'

'I found out about your unofficial transfer enquiry.' Part of her job involved personnel postings and the like. She also held the rank of captain.

I had been to see Sam to sound him out on permanently transferring into the Air Corps, thereby allowing me to continue in aviation at the end of my three-year tour rather than being posted back to military engineering, but I knew the chances were not good due to my age; I was nearing 32 years old. You had to be at least an 'average' graded pilot and be recommended by a squadron commander. I had never failed a test.

'It doesn't look like there are vacancies in your age group, I mean that must be disappointing right?' She blurted out what I already suspected would be the answer.

'Well, you could say that…' I answered, reeling from the unfairness and perceived injustice of my situation.

That moment was pivotal. It was clear - to continue flying, I would have to leave the Army.

# 11

# City Lights

Five hundred feet above County Down, I am struggling with the controls of ZA730, and I am in a serious situation. Glancing at the Central Warning Panel, the amber HYD caption has illuminated indicating that the pressure in the hydraulic system which powers the flying controls has fallen below a critical level. The collective lever in my left hand has risen up of its own accord and I am pushing down hard to maintain a descending flight path while in my right hand, the cyclic has a mind of its own and is becoming stiff to operate and hold. Due to my over-controlling the Gazelle is rocking from side to side. Reducing speed will help, I thought, as I search in front of the nose for somewhere to put down.

Down below, a couple of miles away is a disused airfield with big grass areas intersected with old concrete runways. No one about as far as I could see. Slowing down to 50 knots now, I have to push forward considerably to prevent the nose rising even further thereby preventing me flying forwards. Surprisingly, the pedals are easy to control now, but I remember from my training that I will not be able to push them at low speed and I will spin out of control if I try to hover. I am going to have to do a running landing on the skids.

I've locked the collective lever in position with the friction control and with my left hand now free, I am able to reach into my flying suit pocket for the emergency cards. Should I put out a Mayday call? My instincts say yes but then do I want every Paddy in the vicinity racing to my 'assistance?' I stay silent. Flicking the cards to HYDRAULIC FAILURE, I quickly scan the advice while preventing the helicopter from becoming more unstable.

'Hydraulics Off.' I check the switch on the collective lever is in the OFF position. If the fluid does miraculously repressurise, I don't want the controls to revert back to normal just as I am about to land this thing on the deck.

'Maximum bank 30 degrees.' I am downwind about a mile from the airfield grass area so I will have to gently turn first to the left and then reverse 180 degrees to position for a running landing into wind. Luckily, there is an old, tattered orange windsock billowing from the far corner like a demented banshee giving me a wind direction.

So far so good, I thought wiping the sweat from my eyes with my free hand.
'Control forces are very heavy below 50 knots.'

OK, I will maintain 50 knots until just before touchdown and then hope the grass will slow me down, so I need about 100 metres unobstructed grass to use as a runway.

Approaching at 50ft now into wind I am committed to land. Grunting with the control forces I resist the instinct to pull up and slow down further to a hover which could be fatal. Pushing down hard on the lever, I force the machine down to the grass, which is now rushing up very fast outside the canopy, keeping the nose as straight as I can. Then crunch, and we are down sliding and rocking back and forth on the uneven soil until with a final pitch forward the helicopter comes to rest about 10 metres from the concrete runway.

'Yeah, well done!' Says John the instructor from the left seat, 'Hold the controls firmly now. I am going to switch the hydraulics back on,' and with a flick of a guarded switch on my collective lever, the controls jerked back into normal sensitive response and the HYD caption on the panel went out.

'Remember to keep checking for signs of fire would not you,' he added. Leaking hydraulic fluid is very flammable on hot surfaces, he reminded me more than once.

We are at RAF Bishops Court, and I am undergoing a Commander's operational check before officially being allowed to authorise myself to fly solo in the province on tasks. Up until now, all my flying has been as part of a two-pilot crew but there are some jobs where the front left seat must be occupied by non-aircrew. In this instance the flying controls are removed from that side ensuring there can be no unintended interference with the flying of the aircraft.

Tucked away in the southeast corner of Northern Ireland, Bishops Court used to be an important radar control and reporting station known as 'Ulster Radar' and was now only in use at weekends as a gliding school. During the week it was an excellent place to do some training away from the operational airfields and was relatively secure. To finish off the sortie, John asked me to have a go at a tactical LWNA let-down. This was a way of getting back down through cloud using no external sources whatsoever, just the Doppler navigation equipment fitted to the AH Mark 1 and required precise accurate flying. We were not expected to memorise this procedure and so I reached for my flip book of aide-memoires that every good pilot carries and turned to the page with the diagram of the procedure. Clipping this page to my left knee with a bulldog clip while I flew the cab with my right hand on the cyclic demanded considerable dexterity and the sweat gathered on my brow while John whistled away in the right seat without a care in the world. John picked a large white cross painted on one of the disused runways and announced, 'That is your landing spot!'

Having climbed now to a simulated safety altitude of 2,000ft above the ground, I overflew the cross and as I did so note the wind direction, which was north-easterly today, about 040 degrees which I would use as my approach heading. Coming around a second time overhead the mark, I slewed up on both switches on the LWNA to save the position as a waypoint. I could now return to this point simply by following a bearing indication and I would know how far away I was by the distance indication in nautical miles. If the LZ (Landing Zone) was completely obscured by clouds, then you would have to input its grid reference manually. As I flew away towards the edge of the airfield, the numbers changed all the while on the display, the distance increasing in value. Turning again and flying outside the disused airfield perimeter now, I adjusted the airspeed to 100 knots and turned back straight and level to the white cross. I set the WP/OFF switch to WP and now my friendly homing pointer appeared on my attitude indicator, so all I had to do was keep the needle in the middle of the instrument and I would be heading directly to my desired landing point. My brain was doing cartwheels thinking ahead to the start of this procedure. Turn downwind once overhead, which I mentally calculated would be 220 degrees, and simultaneously descend to 1,500ft until I was three miles away from the spot. I turned and lowered the collective to set up a gradual descent. Scanning the BRG/DIST display until it read three miles, I then turned the helicopter 45 degrees to port so 175 degrees on the direction indicator and hit the stopwatch.

Maintain 1,500ft.

After 40 seconds of this and my brain exploding with concentration, I banked right in what is called a rate one turn which to us aviators means three degrees per second or approximately 15 degrees bank at this speed, all the way back round to centre the homing needle again at 040 degrees into wind and pointing back at the LZ. I had reversed direction successfully now to get down! During the turn I remembered to display groundspeed and drift on the computer, so as I rolled out I reduced speed to 60 knots over the ground; about 75 knots on the airspeed indicator. At three miles, I lowered the collective to set up a 500-foot-per-minute rate of descent, meaning in simple maths, I would hit the ground in three minutes! 60 knots groundspeed also means one mile a minute, so I would reach the LZ in three minutes. Simple maths but juggling all these calculations while flying the cab was a real challenge. The radio altimeter had been set to 200ft earlier, so if I could not see the LZ visually by then, I would execute what is known as a go-around, or overshoot as the RAF like to call it.

Keep the needle centred.

My first approach was smack on heading, but I had descended too fast and fallen short of the designated landing spot. However, after a second attempt which was tidier, I was declared match fit and we headed for home at low level, skirting the sandy shores of beautiful Strangford Lough. Avoiding Newtownards Airfield to the east, John pulled the helicopter up to transit over Belfast City and on to our next destination: Palace Barracks.

Palace Barracks at Holywood was the main Army base in Belfast and home to City Flight, a small detachment of Gazelle AH1s whose role was to provide top cover for the numerous patrols criss-crossing the city from the many small fort-like security locations scattered around the capital. It was the easiest HLS (Helicopter Landing Site) to land on. The barracks square was well-lit with no obstructions. Apart from being really secure, the only hazard was that it was very close to Belfast City regional airport. They had very few arrivals and departures in any case from the short runway in the docklands area although I believe it is much busier now.

The flying was much different here with a lot of high hover flying and slow orbits following up incidents or reports from the ground. Two minutes to go, and I announced our arrival using the HLS designator 'Papa Zero One Two' and we settled down inside the compound.

John had the dubious pleasure of doing flying checks on two of the pilots based there. Known as a 'six-monthly', every pilot had to perform a handling check with an instructor demonstrating that you could were still a proficient aviator. It usually involved a confined area landing somewhere challenging as well as the ubiquitous 'engine-off' landing to conclude the test. This was going to take the best part of the rest of the day so I was cleared solo back to Aldergrove. John would fly back as a passenger using one of the City Flight's cabs later that day.

Palace Barracks dates back to 1886, when the War Office bought a bishop's palace – hence the name – from the Church of Ireland for £1,000. Why was it built? One factor may have been the serious sectarian violence which erupted in Belfast in 1886 in the wake of the Home Rule Bill, unrest that required increased police and military resources to contain it.

I was back the very next day. A pilot had reported sick, and I was tasked with an E4A one-hour sortie with a pick-up at Palace Barracks on call at one hours' notice, which meant ready to go at Aldergrove to be there at the appointed time. I spent the early part of the day checking the weather on the BBC weather bulletins as extraordinarily strong winds were forecast that day, gusting to 40 knots. The Gazelle had a windspeed limitation on starting and stopping rotors of 40 knots. I eventually got a call at 11.30 from Ops at Aldergrove and after drawing my weapon from the armoury with a signature and signing for the Gazelle with another, I walked out alone across the pad to my assigned cab. It felt weird after so many flights as two crew to be alone and entrusted with this mission. The Gazelle is after all a single pilot helicopter designed to be operated by one pilot occupying the right seat, but two pairs of mark one eyeballs were usually better than one. The rotors were tied down but at least she was facing into wind and soon enough, I had the walkaround completed and was glad to get onboard and out of the fresh wind blowing across the lough. I checked my watch, I had already used up 22 minutes of my one hour just getting 100 metres to the cab. I had better get a move on or they might have to cancel the Op. Support to the police in airborne surveillance and photo reconnaissance was classed as special operations and E4A were no exception. This was a sub-division of RUC Special Branch responsible for covert surveillance province wide.

I called for start-up requesting a south-west departure. I was number two to a Wessex from 72 Squadron and in turn I crabbed across sideways to the departure spot keeping the Gazelle facing into the wind, twitchy on the pedals now as I steadied the hover and completed the final take-off checks.

'Army Air 328 surface wind Two Six Zero Thirty knots, you are cleared to depart south-west, Special VFR, Call Sandy Bay and remain south of runway 25.'

I repeated the instructions back to the controller. The Gazelle was already in forward flight maintaining the hover. On a calm day with the controls positioned as they were at that split moment, I would have been flying forward with 30 knots airspeed showing, so all I had to do was pull in a little more power today to get away. Days like this were great to fly! Running down the east side of Lough Neagh, I soon passed a picturesque bay curling the side of the large lake and I made my report to Aldergrove Tower who passed me on to the approach frequency with a cheery 'Good luck!' Sandy Bay was another one of Ulster's forgotten airfields.

The airfield was built during the Second World War as a seaplane base. It comprised 12 moorings for flying boats, with extra moorings for attendant vessels. Another four moorings were available to the east of Rams Island, which provided shelter from the prevailing westerly winds. Navigation buoys were laid out to the north and south of Rams Island to guide the flying boats onto the open lough. Like many other Northern Irish airfields, the station was used to let pilots and crews practice bombing and gunnery techniques. From May 1944 it also served as an airport for flights between the UK and the USA. The main users were the US Naval Transport Service and RAF Transport Command, both operating PB2Y Coronados. The aircraft flew from Sandy Bay via Port Lyantey in North Africa and RAF Darrell's Island in Bermuda to the United States or Puerto Rico. The service was well used with a recorded 280 passengers in June 1944 alone. Still, the service ceased on 16 October 1944. The facilities at the airfield were spartan, and flight control was performed from nearby RAF Langford Lodge. Banking east, I picked up the telecommunications mast on Divis Mountain standing sentinel over the city and made my standard 'Ops Normal' call on Tac VHF.

I was about to re-enter the sectarian melting pot of the city of Belfast, with its Orange and Green areas indistinguishable from the air as I flew at top speed over the large basaltic moorland shadowing the city, both closed to the public and out of bounds to the resident troops at that time.

I shut down on the barrack square and climbing out of the Gazelle, I breathed in the city aroma while I walked around to see if anything had fallen off the cab or it had taken any damage. It sounds crazy but the noise of the helicopter was so great that it was impossible to tell if you had been fired at by anything, so it was always a clever idea to have a customary check over for any dings or strike marks. Often in the bad old days of the 1970s when pot shots were far more common, the first pilots knew they had been shot at was after they landed, and a report came in from nearby troops on the ground by telephone.

By now E4A had accurate intelligence on the structure and membership of PIRA's upper echelons in the city and a substantial number of the lower echelons known as the 'red lighters.' The difficulty was always going to be catching them in compromising situations and airborne surveillance was one tool in their armoury. The problem came when the presence of a helicopter overhead would alert an operation in progress and cause it to be cancelled. It was a deadly game of cat and mouse being played out daily. It was not always the IRA however: the UDA (Ulster Defence Association) and UVF (Ulster Volunteer Force) had stepped up their assassination attacks on Catholics in West Belfast and were also being watched too. The accumulation of weapons was only a means to an end for the paramilitaries involved in the deadly business of targeting Republicans, but however they got hold of firearms, they were then faced with hiding, transporting, and maintaining them. Most of the training was done by ex-servicemen or regrettably in some cases, by members of the UDR. The Czech-made VZ.58 was the weapon of choice of both the UVF and UDA and was used in scores of killings and attempted murders. Resembling an AK-47 Kalashnikov, it was a gas-operated assault rifle firing the same 7.62mm round.

Two operators left the ops room from a building on the side of the square and approached. Both in blue jeans and dark jackets, one was carrying a small rucksack while the other had a couple of cameras slung from his shoulders and looked like a news reporter. I was surprised to see they had short crew cut football supporter type haircuts. Introducing themselves with a handshake, the older guy spoke with a normal north England accent while the cameraman had the familiar Ulster twang.

Jim and Andy were running a surveillance op in the Falls, Jim had a pair of stabilised binoculars in his rucksack, and I spotted an MP5 machine pistol with the magazine removed. 'Just in case we come down in the Ballymurphy,' Jim laughed, catching my eye. The Ballymurphy Estate was a notoriously bad place to be seen in uniform but had a few sports fields dotted around large enough to carry out an emergency landing in if the shit hit the fan, so to speak. I set out my ground rules.

'Your call on the operational requirement but if I have any issues on the flying you are asking me to do, I will scrub it. No flying below 1,500ft otherwise I will be breaking the law and you will have to arrest me,' I said jokingly. 'I can only hold a hover into wind today which means we will have to position right of your target, so you get a better view.'

Jim and Andy concurred and shared snippets of the operation. The need-to-know basis of information was duly applied and after reminding Jim where to plug in the gyro-binoculars, I started up and went through all the functional tests more conscientiously than before. After all, I now had paying passengers! I was asked to head towards the Springmartin area of West Belfast, specifically the Orange Hall, which Jim would point out to me when we got there. I called Belfast City Airport, less than a kilometre away, before lifting to check if they had any arrivals or departures. Nothing, then after adjusting my altimeter to the local pressure setting, I lifted and flew south-west over the urban jungle of streets and flats towards our target. A new Belfast had evolved in the 10 years since I had foot patrolled and driven around the city. Much of the violence of the Troubles had taken place in the streets and suburbs of Belfast and Derry; the Falls, Divis Street, New Lodge, Ardoyne, Tiger Bay, and Short Strand were traditional terraced workers' housing. Much of this had been cleared away and replaced by new housing developments with small gardens and three or four bedrooms, however, the sectarian divide still existed in these bright new areas. Further south-west, the Ballymurphy Estate, Turf Lodge, Andersonstown and Twinbrook were contrasting modern post-war council housing estates with box-style smaller tower blocks and maisonettes and where the roulement companies used to patrol from fort-like security bases.

Jim and Andy just needed a quick 15 minutes on task. An informer had flagged up weapons hides at the centre, and this had been put under surveillance for the previous week, but they needed some additional photographs and information to give the ground teams details of hidden exits or parking spots. One thing that was at risk was alerting the bad guys to the fact that the location was under surveillance, so often a 'dummy location' would be used in tandem with the primary one so that it was less likely the prime target might be compromised. Our dummy location was given to be the leisure centre nearby, so they focussed on that particular car park while I planned a forced landing there should the engine fail. It was while we were over our alternate target that a call came in on Jim's RUC earpiece that a van matching the description of one under surveillance had parked up in broad daylight at the centre, and could we take a closer look to verify the occupants. A helicopter hovering overhead at 1,500ft is fairly conspicuous, so I set up a left-hand slow orbit banking all the time so that both officers had the best view possible from their seats, but to no avail as no one approached the van and, as far as Jim could make out, it was unoccupied. We flew around for a while, and I did question in my mind the usefulness of airborne surveillance in such a densely populated area from this height, but they both seemed pleased at the information they had gathered from a different perspective anyway.

The mechanics of holding a high hover were no different to hovering just above the ground but tended to follow a predictable sequence. I would locate the target area and rather than try to come to a stop directly overhead would creep forward from about a kilometre slowly, at about 10 to 15 knots, until finding the best position for the observer or camera operator when I would pull in power on the collective and raise the nose gently to bleed off the final few knots of airspeed. This was possible for a few minutes at a time, but inevitably a rate of descent would develop visible on the vertical speed indicator (VSI), the needle would drop from the horizontal and perhaps read one or two notches south. Pulling in more power and easing the nose forward just a touch usually slowed the descent but then the pedals would become very twitchy, and the nose would yaw from side to side making the observer's task very difficult. This gyration could morph into a rapid descent, such as a vortex ring state when the helicopter descends in its own downwash becoming uncontrollable, so it was advisable not to let this continue for too long. In your favour was the joy that in the creeping hover into wind, the downwash was being blown downwind and it became a little easier to maintain. Oh, for a stabilised augmentation system and two engines please!

I got back to Aldergrove utterly exhausted, partly due to the blustery flying conditions and also the stress of doing the entire mission solo. How do you explain your shortcomings to yourself? Do you criticise others so easily when you really know yourself? Perfection is unobtainable and flying especially so, that to answer these questions demands a leniency that not everyone can muster. I needed a drink that Saturday night and as I entered the mess, I could hear a party getting underway in the bar. I cautiously sneaked a look to see who was in there, intending to get changed first, but to no avail. Dom had spotted me from behind and dragged me in to the fray. I made a beeline for Izzie and after a hefty gin and tonic danced to the B52s repeatedly until I staggered off to bed exhausted.

## 12

# The Wild West

I met Steve, the Royal Green Jackets pilot, one morning in the mess and we walked out together to the bus that would take us to the squadron hangar. 'Hey, did you hear about Dom? He was doing some golf practice near the barracks guardroom, and he fizzed one over the high fence by accident, made a heck of a racket. The ops room guy thought they were under attack and stood the whole company to. Even the guys resting were up rushing around. Hilarious!' I laughed thinking of Dom shouting 'fore' at the compound as he watched in horror as his ball sailed away in the Ulster wind. Needless to say, all golf practice was stopped in the barracks after this incident.

It was the middle of May and I had been on tour here now for nearly four months with only a couple of weeks flying left. I was starting to get expectation fatigue, a tiredness due to the constant threat of the possibility of being shot at and hearing reports of incidents happening to other units around the province on the incident net. The reminder was the physical routine of the daily signing out and in of weapons as a matter of routine. After all, who goes to work normally sat in an armoured seat with a chest protector, two guns and field dressing kits hidden away in your pockets? Remembering to wear your ID tag around your neck was another daily reminder of the strange existence we all lived.

I was pleased that day to learn that I would be flying with Staff Dave Newell to provide top cover for Steve's Lynx helicopter as he conducted troop insertions around Enniskillen for the Fermanagh Roulement Battalion. We were both aircraft commanders but Staff Newell being the senior pilot got the left seat and the authorisation due to the quirks of rostering. Steve's ship would be doing all the interesting take-offs and landings while we hovered overhead observing. There would inevitably be a lot of waiting around as there always was working with the infantry as plans were often changed at the last minute or delayed for some reason or another.

Battalion HQ, and three companies were located in the old airfield of St Angelo near to Enniskillen. Two other companies were at the RUC Station in Lisnaskea, which also housed a UDR company.

The role of the battalion was to support the RUC in maintaining law and order. The main opposition was an experienced IRA Active Service Unit operating from the

Republic of Ireland which was supported by local IRA members. The threat from the IRA was the usual mixture of shootings, proxy-bombs, and landmines on roads. The latter was a real threat and patrols were told not to walk on roads, especially near to the border. In the 18 months preceding the battalion's tour, the IRA had engaged in almost an 'ethnic cleansing' campaign along the border, killing and attempting to murder Protestants, many either UDR soldiers or police officers, who lived in often isolated farms. The aim was to drive Protestants from the border areas. The Security Forces had responded by mounting a number of operations and creating a number of Permanent Vehicle Check Points (PVCPs) on border roads. Initially the soldiers were living in trenches at these PCVPs, but by the time I arrived in the province all were much more solid structures akin to forts. The PVCP was a key tool in preventing the free movement and smuggling of weapons, ammunition, and people across the border between North and South. They were often joint RUC/Army operations set up on main trunk routes in border regions. They were also isolated and vulnerable to attack. As permanent fortifications, they could be constructed from more durable materials. One sangar design that appears to have been used frequently in PVCPs was the single aperture sangar.

One of the companies was responsible for patrolling the area south-west of Lisnaskea. They manned a number of PVCPS such as at Wattle Bridge. Another company was responsible for the Mullan Bridge VCP where there had been contacts in the past, with fire being returned and the commander was mentioned in dispatches for this action. There was a company responsible for patrolling Lisnaskea and the area to the south-east. This company manned a number PVCPs such as at Annaghmartin and Derryard, with the Anti-Tank Platoon under command based in the RUC station in Rosslea, which was a strong Republican village close to the border. The final company was responsible for the border area to the west up to and including Belleek, the most westerly police station in the United Kingdom.

If there was a title for the most picturesque airfield in Northern Ireland, or even in the world for that matter, it must surely go to St Angelo, three miles north of Enniskillen. It served as the main forward operating base for aviation in the west of the province. During the Second World War, the military made use of the large lakes and access to the Atlantic coast through the Donegal Corridor. British, American, and Canadian airmen served in Co. Fermanagh at wartime airfields such as RAF Castle Archdale and RAF Killadeas.

We took off as a pair, the Lynx leading us out over the lough for the 52-mile flight to St Angelo, or *Golf One Zero Zero*, in the wild west of Ulster. This was long haul flying and with the inevitable westerly 20 knot headwind would reduce our groundspeed to about 100 knots or less, meaning a 30-minute flight, or so we thought. We had opted to transit at 2,500ft, no point in making life difficult for ourselves, and with the summer approaching and the sun heating the canopy like a greenhouse, it was great to get in some cooler air for a change.

Formating on the Lynx now was my primary task and one that would require really accurate flying. I positioned to the left and behind Steve's ship so I could maintain the best overall view and perspective of relative speed. We have nothing electronic in the cockpit to help, just sighting through a section of our window and keeping it in the same place on the Lynx seems to help. The sun is glinting across the lough and the ripples at the shore turned to clearly defined waves in the centre with large dark patches of pressure. We are rocked around by the turbulent air, sometimes speeding up and at other times falling behind. The techniques are different to flying an aeroplane. If a gust picks me up and lifts me higher than I want to fly, or I need to avoid another object such as a bird, then I smoothly lower the collective lever, I do not push the cyclic forward to dive. A push over results in a low-g condition which rotor blades dislike. The effect can be catastrophic in certain helicopters, leading to an unintended roll to the right and the rotor head striking the mast head. The Gazelle was not prone to this due to the nature of the three-bladed design but unloading and reloading the disc rapidly is never a good idea and one instilled during our training.

I concentrated on the airspeed and the vertical speed indicators. Dave was keeping an eye on the map, checking our lead cab was on the right course – which it was – and I remember hearing Steve saying he wanted to overfly Omagh, a slight deviation from a straight-line route, in case there were any problems. The county we were flying over was Tyrone and it was all quiet on the western front so far. There was a feeling that the situation was developing into a stalemate. The horror of the Enniskillen Remembrance Day bombing in 1987 had lost the IRA a lot of support at grass roots level and it was inevitable they would have to resort to such atrocities to try and win an unwinnable war.

'Sir, take the VHF comms; I've got a call coming in on VHF Tac,' Dave chirped up, and I continued concentrating hard on keeping up with Steve, who appeared to be gaining ground again. I was already at IPS – the intermediate pitch stop on the collective – meaning I had raised it to the normal maximum detent for cruise flight. If Steve flew any faster, I would have to politely remind him to slow down but I knew he would love that. It wasn't actually Steve flying; he was the Aircraft Commander today and had a corporal pilot as his driver. New to the AAC, the army accepted corporals as pilots, but they had to attain the rank of sergeant before going on a commander's course at Middle Wallop; another 15 hours of tactical training and a conversion to flying from the left seat. We were still at 2,500ft, out of range of small arms fire but not from surface-to-air guided missiles. How many had the Fermanagh ASU got hold of? I bet someone in the intelligence empire knew but we hadn't a clue. Steve had his ALQ-144 IR jammer fitted and running and the suppression equipment on the twin exhausts, the first stage deflecting the hot gases 90 degrees downwards and the second stage allowing outside air to cool and shield the efflux.

'Staff… ask him what indicated speed Corporal Trevalyan is flying at.' I was still falling behind. 'He says they are doing 110 knots as agreed,' Dave answered after a short communication with the Lynx. After a while Steve transmitted an apology, he had forgotten that the exhaust suppressors had the effect of making the airspeed indicator underread by about 10 knots, so in reality the Lynx had been travelling at 120 knots through the air while we in the Gazelle could only maintain about 110 knots. This was partly due to the aerodynamic drag resulting from the stores boom and the ancillary equipment that we carried; namely the FINCH camera pod and the Nitesun searchlight.

An RAF Wessex became visible lower down to our left heading for some landing site in the border area. I gave a 'Morning' courtesy call on FSC (Flight Safety Common) on the Ultra High Frequency radio but received no answer. Probably busy I thought, but I was interrupted by Dave again to my left, 'Sir, looks like we are being re-tasked, standby.'

'Roger that' I acknowledged back. Dave was the senior pilot left seater and would make any tactical or aviation decisions. Despite having over double my flying hours, he also had been in-theatre longer, making up one of the permanent members of the squadron. He knew his stuff, but would he make the right assessments today? We had a saying 'You are only as good as your last flight,' meaning you can have a great reputation as a pilot, but it can vanish with one cock-up. The pressure was internal, and we all put ourselves through it, call it a code of conduct if you like.

We were over Omagh and were now on the last leg down towards Angelo. Tappaghan Mountain at 1,100ft was on our right and the outline of Upper Lough Erne stretching towards Belleek came into view. Dave broke in on the intercom, 'I've got VHF comms again, it looks like a foot patrol has gone missing down near the border.'

'Gone missing?' I queried the definition.

'One of the patrol bases, possibly the Parachute Regiment, has lost communications with a foot patrol and a second callsign in the multiple cannot raise them either. What's more is they heard two gunshots from the last known area of the patrol. They have been out of comms for two hours now. Aldergrove ops got alerted because we are in the area and have raised this as a high priority task.'

Lost communications with a patrol was a serious situation and needed to be followed up and investigated. My immediate thoughts were of the guys on the ground and how vulnerable they were.

'Surely the other multiple must know where they are?' I suppose it could be a simple map reading error, but these guys knew the ground quite well. There had to be another reason that this situation had developed and there was the gunfire report…

Dave continued, 'We are to continue as a pair down to Angelo and get more details from the local battalion operations net and be prepared to go and look for them.' Steve had slowed up and we reduced our speed in tandem partly to save fuel and partly to allow Dave to plot all the map references he had been given from the signaller at Aldergrove. The plan then evolved around Steve continuing to Angelo to save valuable flying hours and fuel while we in the Gazelle would set course for the missing patrol and try and find them using our FLIR (Forward Looking Infrared) camera system. This was a sound plan in my estimation and made best use of the available resources. The Lynx could be used to ferry a Quick Reaction Force as back up from Angelo if required.

My parent unit back in England, in the sleepy hollow known as Netheravon, was 658 Squadron. Motto: 'Videmus Delemus' (We See and Destroy!) The squadron's role was to support 5 Airborne Brigade in Out of Area Operations worldwide and we sent Gazelles and Scouts to support their exercises in the UK and elsewhere. 2nd Battalion, The Parachute Regiment were one of the four battalions in the brigade and many peacetime tasks involved flying the Brigade Commander on recces or casualty evacuation near to a DZ (Drop Zone) after a live drop. We all wore a DZ flash of light blue over blue on our combat uniform. I felt on home ground and looked forward to supporting my Para colleagues, although they wouldn't know it was a 5 Brigade pilot looking for them of course. 'Sir, head 180 degrees initially and head for the A4 down to Lisnaskea and we will use that to get a steer.' My primary task was, of course lookout, while Staff Dave buried himself in 1:50,000 scale maps approximately equal to one inch to one mile. I noticed some angry looking clouds approaching from the west. Oh no not again, I thought. We are going to need good visibility to find these blokes.

'Have fun Gazelle Five, see you at *Golf One Zero Zero*.' Steve went off frequency to liaise on his task with the battalion and left us to it. The border area of Fermanagh we were headed for was tucked to the west of the Monaghan salient and was characterised by the scores of lakes comprising Upper Lough Erne and others. Poorly drained and with numerous streams and ditches, it must have been a nightmare to negotiate on foot without sticking to roads and tracks but that is exactly how to get yourself killed in Ireland. From Lisnaskea, we flew down to Newtonbutler and circled a while at 1,500ft to get a better look around. I went through some options. There was a real risk of a blue-on-blue incident here if patrols did not know where each other were precisely located. The two shots fired might have been unconnected with the missing patrol but might equally well have been a contact on the patrol or initiated by the patrol itself. We just didn't have enough information at the moment, but it was not our job to fight the war at this stage, just to win the battle, as the saying went. Staff Dave warmed up the FLIR camera on the starboard boom. I concentrated on looking out for weather and hostile activity. In this part of Fermanagh large white crosses had been painted on the minor roads at the border, used as a marker for helicopters. More information came through, the area was Rosslea Forest, grid reference H540535, that's a 10,000 square metre area of country to start with. From above, a human occupies less than one square metre of the Earth's surface. Deep joy. Our plan was to talk one of the patrols – Papa One Zero Charlie – onto the other one without them killing each other in a firefight. I turned east and flew the 10 or so miles towards the border village of Rosslea and the PVCP at Annaghmartin. We had to hurry and get this done. Our fuel state was not infinite, and the shadows of clouds darkened the verdant fields and loughs scattered below. Patchwork quilt; Irish style. The forest was an obvious place to bivvy out in overnight and the patrols' tasks would probably be to talk to locals, check cars and locate possible mortar firing points. For these elite infantry soldiers, it was better than being cooped up inside a cramped patrol base or RUC station with all the base duties to piss them off. Each brick within a multiple carried an electronic countermeasures pod to alert for radio control signals that could detonate a device buried in the undergrowth.

No further than the small hill to the west of the forest was the border with the Irish Republic and I used this as my reference point and slowed into a 180-degree left turn for Dave to have a closer look. Immediately he spotted a foot patrol on the edge of a small track leading into the trees from the north just outside the village, and confirmed this was Papa One Zero Charlie on the Cougar net, and that the missing callsign was Papa One Zero Delta. 'Why don't they just walk back in?' pondered Dave, referring to the latter callsign. I was inclined to agree but we didn't even know they were capable of that. All the time the cloud base was lowering, it wouldn't be long before we would not be able to maintain 1,500ft and be forced to revert to low-level flying where the camera would be little or no use. I hovered slap bang over the large coniferous forest criss-crossed with firebreaks while Staff Dave scanned below. They had to be in there somewhere, but another thought sprang to mind, perhaps an injury had prevented them from returning immediately to a pre-agreed rendezvous point.

Papa One Zero Charlie relayed that the gunfire they had heard a while back sounded like it had come from inside the forest but there were scattered small holdings along the area which could have been the source. I started to think this was not the real issue and was just a coincidence. This incident shows just how important short-range communications are in rural areas and spare batteries are no good if they haven't been charged properly.

There was a clearing at the southern edge of the forest which reminded me of the one in Harewood Forest near Wallop that we used for training; just large enough for one Gazelle to drop into. 'I think this could be them,' keyed Dave on the intercom, pointing a green finger at the screen. Three blobs of white were moving around the edge of the clearing with a fourth – presumably the machine gunner – about 50 yards away lying down. It's either them or a bloody IRA patrol about to ambush, and although out of small arms range descending lower might mean a brief and unpleasant encounter with an M60 machine gun. After scribbling the grid reference of the clearing on his kneepad, Staff Dave slewed the position in on the LWNA and we cleared off to the north. I had already inadvertently entered cloud briefly once before, immediately regaining visual contact with the ground, a very unnerving experience. The weather had taken the option away to hold a secure position over the forest and a descent to below 150ft would serve little purpose. Our task was to find the patrol and report the location. We had found an unconfirmed unit but, in my mind, it was Papa Zero One Delta. No point risking a repeat of the Derrygore Gazelle shooting. The other mobile would have to patrol south through the forest and rendezvous with these guys one way or another. They were armed and at least they could defend themselves if fired upon, we could not.

We held overhead to the west of Rosslea for as long as we could, but the cloud base was down too below 1,000ft now and it seemed inevitable that providing top cover was no longer going to be possible, so after reporting the situation to Angelo Ops, we were told to return for refuel. My fellow pilot flew the 20 miles back to Angelo and completed a perfect approach to the old airfield. We parked near to a Wessex at the far end of the long tarmac runway near a blast wall. There was no sign of Steve's Lynx, which was out doing the previously planned resupply missions.

One of three airfields on the shores of Lough Erne, the others being RAF Killadeas and RAF Castle Archdale, St Angelo was home in 1943 to one of my favourite aircraft: the Consolidated PBY Catalina, hunting enemy submarines with RAF Coastal Command. The designation 'PBY' was determined in accordance with the US Navy aircraft designation system of 1922; 'PB' representing 'Patrol Bomber' and 'Y' being the code assigned to Consolidated Aircraft as its manufacturer. Although slow and ungainly, Catalinas distinguished themselves in the Second World War. Allied forces used them successfully in a wide variety of roles for which the aircraft was never intended. PBYs are remembered for their rescue role, in which they saved the lives of thousands of aircrews downed over water. Catalina pilots called their aircraft the 'Cat' on combat missions and 'Dumbo' in air-sea rescue service. I wonder what these austere veteran aviators would make of our Gazelle's nickname, the 'whistling chicken-leg?'

After shutting down and grabbing a bite to eat in the canteen, usually a greasy NI burger, we found out more of the jigsaw puzzle. The patrol commander had mistakenly taken out some partially charged PRC radio batteries instead of fully charged ones. They had not enough power to transmit and could only receive intermittent transmissions, including ours. They had not wanted to give away their position with smoke or strobe lights for obvious reasons, being so close to the border. As their other multiple approached through the forest, the patrol commander took a chance and shouted a password to his multiple commander before getting a right royal rollocking. The shots came from a farmhand dealing with rabbits. We were thanked for our efforts, and I left the ops room thinking of a more effective procedure for dealing with this situation in the future.

My reward for our illustrious performance in Fermanagh was to be tasked for Gazelle Two the following day, the cab assigned to the Commander Land Forces (CLF) in Northern Ireland. I inspected the cab with the REME line dispatcher when I got back to Aldergrove and made sure it was fully serviceable and the flying controls on the left side had been removed. The CLF had responsibility for all three brigades, had access to the politicians making the decisions in Westminster, and answered to the General Officer Commanding, a lieutenant general. It went remarkably well, and I logged 3.5 hours ferrying him and his Chief of Staff to Enniskillen and then onto the new patrol base at Gortmullan, again right on the border. The landing site at Enniskillen was inside the large RUC complex in the centre of the town near the castle. It was suitable for most types and consisted of a circular 25-metre concrete pad within a 30 metre by 60 metre walled compound surrounded by 20-foot steel fencing. The hazards were numerous; buildings atop high ground 250 metres to the north and north-east, two large church spires up to 75ft a couple of hundred metres to the south and for good measure, a 125-foot mast only a seven-iron distance to the west. If you missed all of these obstacles, then an engine failure would put me and my modern major general into the cold waters of the River Erne. I approached from the north-west hopping over the power cables on short final with my career on the line and noticed I was slightly downwind because it took an awful amount of power to hover, and I nearly embarrassed myself by the potential for a firm touchdown.

VIP flights always involved a lot of waiting around, so after shutting down I unloaded my weapon and walked to see if I could get hold of a telephone line to Aldergrove to get an update on the weather for the return flight, while the CLF visited the local RUC commander. Enniskillen had given its name to two regiments: one infantry; the Royal Inniskilling Fusiliers, and one cavalry; the 5th Royal Inniskilling Dragoon Guards. Enniskillen Castle features on the cap badge of both regiments. The town itself had been relatively quiet since the dreadful bombing three years earlier. After a mercifully uneventful flight back to HQ at Lisburn, I returned to Aldergrove for my last flight that day and during my tour. It was a tracking and balance air test in XZ346. I hope this airframe is still flying today.

It was time to return my LCJ and chest protector to the store, hand back my weapons card used for authorisation to draw weapons from the armoury, and get my logbook signed by the management. I had logged 180 hours flying, approximately a third of that total had been at night. Izzie had kindly offered to drop me off to get the RAF Tristar flight back to Brize Norton the next day. It was the last time I saw her or Northern Ireland.

# 13

# Ops Normal

And so, it was over. Another tour of Northern Ireland but a different one seen from a new and almost detached perspective. Not one mile walked in urban jungle or blackthorn hedge used as cover this time around. I fell back into the squadron routine at Netheravon, took some leave, saw some friends, and reconciled a feeling of regret that the experience had been too short, too inconclusive, almost meaningless. I had done my duty; I had done everything asked of me but strangely enough I wanted more. I was just becoming good at the job, but the Army system always posts you onwards at peak proficiency. I busied myself that July preparing for a squadron exercise supporting the brigade up in Scotland at RAF West Freugh. We did loads of low-level recces in Low Flying Area 16 looking for potential large helicopter landing sites for company-strength insertions and also for smaller anti-tank firing points. It was pleasant to fly without the need to carry weapons and ammunition and the only enemy up here was the Scottish weather and the occasional large buzzard.

It was during the next month that events eclipsed any further news of the Troubles. On 2 August 1990, the Iraqi military invaded the neighbouring State of Kuwait, and had fully occupied the country within two days. I was put on 48 hours' notice to move and even got vaccinated in preparation for deployment to Iraq with an all-arms advance party from 5 Brigade. Subsequently 1 Armoured Division in Germany was mobilised instead and the lightly equipped airborne brigade never deployed in the Gulf War despite the enticing prospect of a full-blown out of area operation to be involved in. Stood down from this looming commitment, I found myself back on normal squadron training maintaining proficiency at instrument flying and the monthly night flying exercise around Salisbury Plain.

A highlight during this period was delivering Gazelle XX309 from deep maintenance back to 664 Squadron in Minden, Germany. This was a flight that took nearly 4 hours with refuel stops at RAF Manston in Kent – where I had experienced my first Chipmunk flight – and RAF Wildenrath near the Dutch/German border. It was my first real international flight as a pilot and talking to all the different ATC controllers was a real experience. During the trip with the squadron 2IC, we talked about my Ireland tour and I asked if I could be rostered another tour next year. He said he would look into it but we were already undermanned as a squadron, so it didn't look likely. Anyway, what was I thinking? More night duties, a repeat performance, an encore, it would never be the same. However, he did suggest using my experience gained there by picking up the tasks that regularly required a Gazelle to support the 14 Intelligence and Security Operators course. It involved flying single pilot to a secret camp near Hereford and flying a sortie with a trainee operator during the photoreconnaissance phase of their six-month course before they were deployed to the 'Det' in Northern Ireland.

When we returned to UK, I volunteered for the next available Task 400 as it was called, and the experience was almost like being in Ireland again. The trainees had already adopted the jeans and long hair look of their predecessors but rarely spoke to me besides instructions about heights and headings. When asked to hover over a village at 500ft however, I did have to politely explain this would not go down well if they asked to do this for real. This was the first of many such flights and I became a regular customer for the remainder of my tour.

Another highlight was the arrival from the United States of the 160th Special Operations Aviation Regiment (Airborne), also known as 'Night Stalkers', on a liaison visit and I got to fly the MH-6M Little Bird, nicknamed the 'Killer Egg.'

Another year went by and my contract with the Army Air Corps was running out. What should I do? An almost certain staff job awaited me in the Royal Engineers. I tried again to transfer but was met with the same reply. No vacancy in your year of birth. The Corps was management heavy, too many officers chasing the nirvana of a second or third flying tour. I took the plunge and applied to leave the Army under voluntary redundancy and that is how I found myself at the controls of a Robinson R22 learning to fly again…

I was about to embark on the second-best achievement in my flying career to date; becoming a civilian flying instructor. First, I had to learn to fly the light helicopter itself, distinctly different from the Gazelle in that it has a piston-engine prone to carburettor icing and has a two bladed rotor driven by a vee-belt pulley. The view from the cockpit however was just as good if not better than the Gazelle and there was even a police version which allowed VFR operation at night with either landing lights or searchlights operable. I went to Fort Lauderdale in Florida to gain the necessary 15 hours Pilot-In-Command required by the Civil Aviation Authority before I could start the course. The R22 had a relatively high number of accidents in the early years. It was not specifically designed to be a trainer but due to the relatively low price and running costs, it inevitably was bought in large numbers by flying schools. The main problem was that the relatively low inertia of the rotor blades could cause the rpm to decay rapidly in the event of an engine failure. Another potential problem was low-G mast bumping accidents that were completely avoidable by good pilot judgement: forward cyclic movement after a pull-up could be fatal, for example.

Mike Green taught me the patter. 'Practice engine failure GO!' became my mantra. There was a plentiful supply of 30-minute trial lessons to be flown which eventually paid back the eye-watering cost of the course. Some were frightened, some were sick, some even went on to complete their Private Pilot's Licence. I stressed to every student to treat this machine with respect and that it wouldn't kill them if they kept to the procedures. There were still accidents, even involving some high-hour instructors, and so inevitably I searched for a flying career in a form of aviation with a higher life-expectancy. It was also during this period that I learnt of the tragic accident at Bessbrook in November 1992 involving an RAF Puma and a Gazelle of 665 Squadron while landing. All four passengers and crew in the Puma were killed and the two Gazelle crew badly injured. I checked my logbook and the Gazelle involved, ZB681 had been one of the last cabs I had flown during my tour.

But what of Northern Ireland? In 1994 The IRA announced a ceasefire, '…as of midnight 31 August, there will be a complete cessation of military operations.' It had accepted that armed struggle alone would not lead to a united Ireland, and it wanted to test the commitment of the British government and unionists to reform through political dialogue.

I felt pleased. Could it be possible that finally after all this time, the Troubles were ending? For me, a certain sort of trouble was beginning. I started having dreams, but one graphic dream kept repeating itself. I was strapped into the Gazelle with the engine running, rotors stopped. In the back were two people, somebody important. I am in a field landing site near the border waiting to start up. Suddenly, a figure is walking towards us from the front on my side of the helicopter. He seems to be carrying something purposely. He could be carrying a grenade. Where was the bloody protection force? He stops about 20 metres away but then approaches again. Who is this guy? 'Do something!' shouts someone in the back. I open my door, unstrap, and draw the Browning 9mm from my LCJ and stepping out shout 'Army helicopter, stop or I fire!' above the noise of the engine. He keeps on walking oblivious. I fire and he goes down. I had this dream so many times, I began to believe it was true. I couldn't mention it to anyone for fear of losing my flying licence, so I got no help. I had started drinking quite a lot: you don't dream in a drunken stupor. I hated myself for having this dream, but it eventually disappeared as quickly as it came.

Despite the ceasefire, the violence continued in Ireland which angered me. The sniper attacks in South Armagh had stopped for a while but there were still sporadic sectarian shootings and bomb attacks elsewhere, culminating in the Docklands bombing in London in 1996.

I was a captain with a regional airline by this time. Our routes included Dublin and Cork and I remember feeling uneasy when required to overnight there in hotels for the first time despite it being perfectly safe.

After the Good Friday Agreement in 1998, the skies became safer and the dismantling of the Golf and Romeo watchtowers by the Royal Engineers began culminating in a massive removal of the dismantled sections by Pumas and Chinooks. On 31 July 2007, the longest continuous deployment of UK Armed Forces came to an end and Operation Banner was over.

# Epilogue

# March 2022

While conducting the research and writing for this book during the lockdown, I discovered two things. Firstly, I had a burning curiosity to revisit Northern Ireland. What was it really like now? How would I be treated as an outsider? Was it possible to go anywhere at will without fear? Secondly, I realised how little I knew then of the Troubles as a whole and the collateral damage it had caused over the years to so many people. Was it really all over now or could it re-emerge from a 20-year slumber ignited by Brexit or a change of US president more sympathetic to Irish unity?

I rewatched the excellent BBC series *Spotlight on the Troubles: A Secret History* with its haunting soundtrack and that spurred my interest even further. It is said that every soldier revisits his battlefield at least once, and so after waiting for all Covid restrictions to be lifted I took an Easyjet flight to Belfast (International) accompanied by my wife. It was a surreal moment touching down on Irish soil after so many years and one thing that struck me was the diversity of my fellow passengers. A young man next to me was reading *Bad Blood: A Walk along the Border* by Colm Toibin. He didn't look old enough to have been born during the Troubles. The book looked interesting.

We picked up our hire car and headed south to join the motorway to Enniskillen, the first stop on our itinerary. The road out of Aldergrove was fast and relatively empty on this Saturday afternoon and I couldn't help noticing the frequency of petrol stations with obscure franchises not present in England and the proliferation of wind turbines dotted around the landscape.

Everything looked so normal, so familiar, so unthreatening.

Arriving in Enniskillen, I took the road up to the airfield and pulled into the car park, now in use as a Covid testing centre! Signs saying 'No photography allowed' were not helpful but I managed to take a couple of photos of the airfield. A light twin-engine aircraft, possibly a Piper, taxied in front of us and disembarked its passengers. The airfield looked vaguely familiar with no evidence of its historical past remaining. We left and parked up in the town. The kind lady at Enniskillen Castle allowed us a quick look around as it had closed for the day, and we walked along the river. We were only plain tourists now as the evening sun dazzled in the low sky.

The next morning, after the best full 'English' breakfast of my life, we visited Castle Coole, now in the hands of the National Trust, and marvelled at the beauty of the lake and grounds in the morning sunshine. We chatted to a lady walking her dog who had only recently returned to Enniskillen after leaving for Australia and Newcastle 'because of the Troubles'. I asked if there were any parts of Northern Ireland she would not consider safe. She replied that there were areas in the cities that she would avoid but due to normal drug related crime, not terrorism.

We drove on to County Armagh. I pulled into Bessbrook, passing the Mill and the former HLS opposite. It was impossible to believe this had once been the busiest helicopter base in Western Europe. The field was undulating and uneven and seemed smaller than I remembered. The derelict terminus of the old Bessbrook and Newry tramway was still there, and I believe there are plans to redevelop the Mill for housing. The highlight of the day was the drive to Slieve Gullion, a journey that would have been unimaginable for me 30 years ago. On the way passing Cloghoge Mountain, former site of the OP I had flown to on numerous occasions, I couldn't help but feel uneasy, an imposter even. The mountain has now been designated an Area of Outstanding Natural Beauty. At the carpark, there were plenty of families enjoying the sunshine, including many cars from the Republic, and the views over South Armagh were terrific. The landscape was dotted with isolated wind turbines now. I wish I had done this earlier, I found myself saying.

Our hotel that evening was the Dunadry Hotel and Gardens, an old friend from the past but before I left Northern Ireland there was one last thing I wanted to see. The next day we boarded the aircraft for the flight home on a blustery grey day, more like the weather I remembered from my tour. As we taxied out for a take-off on Runway 17, out of the window I caught a glimpse of a solitary Gazelle on a pad outside a hangar, rotors tied down against the wind, and I imagined myself all those years ago walking across the tarmac removing the straps, stowing my gear, and climbing in to flick the battery master on, to hear the familiar whine in the headset and to set off on another adventure to defend the peace.

# Appendix

# Early Day Motion

## Helicopter Pilots During the Troubles in Northern Ireland

EDM 1479: tabled on 03 July 2018

That this House thanks the helicopter pilots who operated during the Troubles in Northern Ireland; recognises their courage and dedication to the job of providing support and back up for soldiers on the ground at the coal face of acts of terrorism against them; and further acknowledges the vital role they played in seeing the defeat of the IRA's war of terror against civilians and the British forces alike.

Signed by:

Mr Jim Shannon MP
Mr Paul Girvan MP
Sir Geoffrey M Donaldson MP
Mr Nigel Dodds MP
Mr Gavin Robinson MP
Mr David Simpson MP
Mr Bob Blackman MP
Sir Peter Bottomley MP
Mr Ian Paisley MP
Sir Mike Penning MP

# Bibliography

## Books
Dewar, Michael, *The British Army in Northern Ireland* (London: Arms and Armour Press, 1996)

English, Richard, *Armed Struggle, The History of the IRA* (London: Pan Macmillan, 2004)

Hall, Malcolm, *From Balloon to Boxkite: The Royal Engineers and Early British Aeronautics* (Stroud: Amberley Publishing, 2010)

Harnden, Toby, *Bandit Country: The IRA and South Armagh* (London: Hodder & Stoughton, 2000)

James, NDG, *Plain Soldiering, A History of the Armed Forces on Salisbury Plain* (Salisbury: Hobnob Press, 1987)

Potter, John, *A Testimony to Courage, The History of the Ulster Defence Regiment 1969–1992* (London: Leo Cooper, 2008)

Urban, Mark, *Big Boys Rules* (London: Faber and Faber, 1992)

Ware, Darren, *A Rendezvous with the Enemy* (Solihull: Helion, 2010)

Warner, Guy, *Army Aviation in Ulster* (Newtownards: Colourpoint, 2004)

## Other Publications and Sources
*Army Air Corps Journal*
*Belfast Telegraph*
*Daily Telegraph*
*Fermanagh Herald*
*Irish Times*
*Ulster Herald*
Gazelle AH1, Aircrew and Operating Manual
*British Army Aviation* (Key Publishing, 2019)
*Operation Banner: An Analysis of Military Operations in Northern Ireland,* Army Code 71842 (Prepared under the direction of the Chief of the General Staff, 2006)
www.cain.ulst.ac.uk
www.hansard.parliament.uk